Harvey Wish is well known for his work in the field of American history. He is the author of *George Fitzhugh, Propagandist of the Old South, Society and Thought in America, Contemporary America,* which received the American History Publication Society's Book of the Month Award, and *The American Historian,* winner of the Ohio Academy of History's annual award as the outstanding historical work of 1960. Dr. Wish is currently Elbert Jay Benton Distinguished Professor of American History at Western Reserve University.

the Negro since Emancipation

edited by
Harvey Wish

Prentice-Hall, Inc.  Englewood Cliffs, N.J.

Current printing (last digit):
12 11 10 9 8 7 6 5 4 3

LIBRARY OF CONGRESS CATALOG CARD NO.: 64:23550

Printed in the United States of America—C. P 61079 C 61080

Contents

Introduction

Leadership, Strategy, Protest

Long before the Negro Revolution of the 1960's, American Negro leaders had firmly established a persistent tradition of resistance—to slavery, to segregation, to schemes of African colonization, and to social discrimination. Negro history books have long told this story, especially those by Carter G. Woodson, but only in recent decades have historians of both races challenged the conventional picture of the passive Negro content to let northern or southern whites decide his destiny and fight his battles. Besides Dr. Woodson and other Negro scholars like John H. Franklin, Charles Wesley, and Rayford Logan, a growing number of white scholars, particularly the liberal southerner C. Vann Woodward, have made studies of the New South dealing with Negro organizations of sharecroppers and emphasizing that formal Jim Crow arose out of legislation that began shortly before 1900; Clement Eaton of the University of Kentucky has illuminated many facets of ante-bellum biracial history; and, on the far left, Herbert Aptheker has convinced many of the frequency of slave insurrections and sabotage, and of the initiative of Negro abolitionists.

Thus Negro history, once as remote from the main stream of American historiography as Jim Crow could make it, has begun to be blended into a national narrative. Increasingly, younger scholars have dealt with a long, unbroken tradition of racial resistance to domination beginning with the innumerable slave-ship mutinies in the Middle Passage from West Africa. It is logical therefore that the freedom movement of the Sixties calls for the awakening Negro people to become acquainted with their activist ancestors.

Even the hopelessness of slave insurrections and plots, which were regularly betrayed by loyal domestics, did not prevent Gabriel Prosser (1800) and Nat Turner (1831) from striking out for freedom in

Virginia, or Denmark Vesey from conspiring in South Carolina (1822). Dedicated Negroes like Frederick Douglass, Sojourner Truth, and William C. Nell were active abolitionists, using the lecture platform, the newspaper columns, or court cases as instruments of action. Unmentioned in the textbooks are the vigorous Negro clubs of Ohio, Massachusetts, and other states, aided by friendly whites, which fought segregation or the denial of educational opportunity. Though they had few ballot privileges, they could rally behind the slogan "Equality before the Law" and hire lawyers like Thaddeus Stevens—often without fee—to defend escaped slaves or eminent counsel like Charles Sumner to fight school discrimination, as in the Roberts Case of 1848 in Boston. Rebels of the Old Northwest protested the Black Laws which barred Negro migrants, forbade Negroes suffrage, denied them jury service, disregarded Negro testimony against whites, segregated black schoolchildren, and utilized a kind of indenture system that resembled slavery. Before the Civil War, gains were made slowly, and occasionally there were setbacks: Defeat in the Roberts Case meant a victory for the principle of separate and equal accommodations that became the legal basis for the *Plessy* v. *Ferguson* decision of 1896.

During the Civil War, southern Negro leaders paid little attention to the Confederate propaganda against Yankees and few consented to go beyond parading in the southern forces. Southern newspapers boasted of the loyal slaves—and some domestics or personal slaves were loyal. However, southern armies had to cope with a fifth column of Negro snipers, insurrectionists, spies, guerillas, and escaping "contraband." They even fought their former slaves on the battlefield, for over 186,000 Negroes were mustered into the Union armies, and despite strong Yankee prejudices which confined most of them to menial tasks, a substantial number fought bravely—as at Milliken's Bend, Louisiana, where a Negro detachment was wiped out in a last-ditch stand to maintain its position as ordered.

When freedom came, a small but able band of Negro leaders was available. Educated southern Negroes who had never been slaves and literate freedmen—the Talented Tenth eulogized in Du Bois's essay—cooperated with the Freedmen's Bureau, which supervised labor contracts, issued relief rations, and set up Negro schools.

Nevertheless, these leaders were handicapped by the fact that the ex-slaves were 90 per cent illiterate and by the efforts of the former master class and its allies to restore the race controls of slavery through Black Codes and strict rules on employment, vagrancy, and residence. As Negroes tended to support the Union occupation armies and the biracial Radical Republican program, conservative southern whites struck back at "Africanization" through the underground Ku Klux Klan, the Knights of the White Camellias, and other terrorist organizations. Convinced that the South would not fully recognize the consequences of defeat and genuine emancipation ("Revisionist" historians believe it was solely a selfish desire to entrench themselves politically), the Radical Republicans set up military rule in the South and created the "carpetbag" legislatures in which Negro leaders played a large but far from dominant part.

The story of the Reconstruction has been drastically revised since Thomas Dixon's racist novel *The Clansman* (1905), which furnished the scenario for the equally racist motion picture *The Birth of a Nation.* While the pre-1914 Columbia University seminars of John Burgess and William Dunning produced Revisionists who condemned the Reconstruction as a corrupt experiment of northern carpetbaggers and their venal Negro tools, some historians of both races refused to accept any historical theories based on the assumption of *inherent* Negro inferiority. Most important was the influence of Carter Woodson, founder of the *Journal of Negro History* and author of innumerable history textbooks, monographs, and articles which encouraged a feeling of pride in the African as well as American past. Woodson's interpretations of Negro historical controversies, illustrating the role of the activist Negro, are included in this anthology. Dr. Du Bois, a Negro leader in the sense that he formulated the intellectual foundations for strategy, emphatically attacked the Burgess-Dunning school in *Black Reconstruction* (1935), showing how Negro leaders contributed to the welfare and educational achievements of the Radical legislatures. Even the conservative Booker T. Washington wrote enthusiastically of the freedmen's crusade for education after the war—as shown in the selection from *Up from Slavery*—although he does not mention that the Radicals expediently dropped the idea of mixed schools and compromised with the expensive dual-school system.

Militant Negro leaders like Frederick Douglass lost some of their ante-bellum allies when even the uncompromising Garrison and other abolitionists refused to make any real fight for equal suffrage (or actually opposed it). Too many Radicals seem to have been won over—as the Revisionists assert—by the desire to use Negro suffrage to keep themselves in power. Something of Douglass' old militancy is seen in the article reproduced here on "Lynch Law in the South."

Northern philanthropy trained various types of Negro leaders and professional men who differed in philosophy and degrees of social action. Even with the best of intentions, the South felt economically unable to match the gifts of biracial missionary agencies, of the great Peabody and Slater educational funds, or (much later) of the Rockefeller, Jeanes, and Rosenwald foundations. Militants like Dr. Du Bois observed that such Negro leaders as Booker T. Washington were selected and directed by white men of power, including presidents and industrialists, and that this contradicted the tradition of the activist Negro. In fact, the educators heading the large Negro colleges or industrial schools were often white, and white administrators chose Negro teachers—too often poor ones—for Negro elementary schools.

Dedicated white southerners like the ex-Bourbon Confederate Jabez L. M. Curry won praise for their devotion to Negro education, but it was hard for Curry to overcome his doubts about the Negro's educability. Another well-intentioned white, ex-President Rutherford B. Hayes of Ohio, who headed the Slater Fund, told an audience in 1890 that the chief and only gift of Negroes was oratory. This former Union Major-General had reassured anxious Negroes during the disputed election of 1876 that their rights would be safer in the hands of the South than in those of the federal government. Yet Hayes offered young W. E. B. Du Bois the grand opportunity for graduate study in Germany only after a Harvard sponsor reassured him that Du Bois was partly of white ancestry.

The death of Frederick Douglass in 1895, the year of Booker T. Washington's Atlanta Compromise, symbolized the shift from the militant strategy of agitation for equal rights to the conservative philosophy of racial segregation in return for jobs. By this time the victory of the "Demagogue" leaders, backed by the southern small farmers, over the well-to-do "Bourbon" planters, merchants, and industrialists had created a new racial crisis. Since the Bourbons very frequently benefited from the Negroes' votes, they tolerated their continued enfranchisement. This group's conservative program of economy, reconciliation with the North, and industrialization reduced but did not actually cut off the Negro schools set up during Reconstruction and permitted many avenues of employment to remain for the blacks—besides the exploitative convict lease system or the chain gang that attracted the economy-minded.

But the Tillman and Vardaman Demagogues who overthrew the Bourbons struck at their foes by disfranchising the Negro through ingenious methods and introduced a rigid Jim Crow system that went far beyond the limited segregation in effect since the Civil War. Too few "respectable" people effectively protested the intimidation of Negroes through mob lynchings, which increased rapidly after 1885, reaching one hundred a year in 1900. The savage Atlanta race riot of 1906 had its full counterpart in the Springfield, Illinois, outbreak of 1908. In that home of Abraham Lincoln, the mob ran wild for days, beating Negroes, lynching several, and driving many out of town. The Supreme Court reflected the current racist temper, which was enhanced by the new European colonialism, and even upheld the Kentucky legislature's act in segregating Berea College, which had long been established to serve both whites and Negroes.

Booker T. Washington, who lived until 1915, was stunned by these racial developments (which led Du Bois and his associates of the Niagara Movement of protest to join with white liberals to form the NAACP); but he continued to sing the praises of industrial education for Negroes and to urge the importance of creating a Negro business class and a strong yeomanry of Negro farmowners. Southern Negro leaders—usually as conservative as he—saw no practical alternative to Washington's alliance with friendly industrialists who provided jobs and philanthropies for Negroes while the unions excluded his race from skilled work. Assuming that most Negroes would continue to live in the rural South, he used Tuskegee Institute as a sort of pilot experiment for a future prosperous Negro peasantry. He was ready to pay the price of accepting absolute segregation and reassured Dixie by counseling southern Negroes to vote Democratic in local elections while remaining Republican on national issues.

Dr. Du Bois did not oppose industrial training for the Negro masses, but he suspected that the "Tuskegee Machine" denied the intellectual potentiality of that Talented Tenth that required a liberal education. As the years passed he came to look upon Booker T. Washington and his vast patronage power as a force pitted against the advance of Negro equality. Thus Du Bois took up the mantle of the old fighting abolitionist Frederick Douglass. But most of his life, he too saw no profit in uniting with organized labor, with the small southern farmer, or with the Communist party, which offered a militant program for Negro rights. As late as 1933, Du Bois wrote emphatically in *The Crisis,* "The capitalists are against mob law and violence and would listen to justice in the long run because industrial peace increases their profits. On the other hand, the white workers want to kill the competition of 'Niggers.' " The alliance with the white middle class remained a constant in Negro strategy.

The NAACP of 1909, an alliance of antisegregationist Negroes, including intellectuals like Du Bois and members of the Niagara Movement of racial protest, attracted idealistic whites of national stature like Jane Addams of Hull House, Oswald Garrison Villard, grandson of the abolitionist and a man remembered best for his transformation of *The Nation* into a formidable organ of social protest, and John Dewey, ever active in such causes. Jewish intellectuals like Joel E. Spingarn, aware of minority group causes, took positions of leadership or played such an active role that in later years the Black Muslims insisted that the NAACP was a Zionist tool. With Du Bois as editor of its chief organ, *The Crisis,* the NAACP agitated for equal rights assured by the Constitution, depended heavily on legal action, and investigated acts of racial discrimination and brutality.

Urbanization, particularly the movement of Negroes to northern cities, profoundly affected the course of Negro adjustment within an integrated American pattern. This movement reached large proportions after the 1880's as industrial opportunities in the fast-growing cities offered escape from static economic conditions and increasing discrimination. Not unimportant were the ravages of the boll weevil, which wiped out extensive acreages of cotton in many states, creating mass unemployment among Negro sharecroppers. As the rural Negro arrived, unskilled and illiterate, he competed with southern and eastern European immigrants for manual jobs. The new Urban League, founded almost at the same time as the NAACP, was not equipped to handle the housing and adjustment problems of the new arrivals.

World War I, the war to make the world safe for democracy, was followed by the Red Summer of 1919 with its housing riots in so many northern cities, especially Chicago, whose Negro population had multiplied because of war needs. Many Negro leaders became disillusioned as a result. Most impressive among successful Negro leaders during this period was Marcus Garvey in Harlem, who claimed that millions had joined his back-to-Africa movement, which offered a belligerent African Zionism and racial hate that suggest some of the nationalist ideas of the later Black Muslims. In fact, although Garvey failed to capture the intellectuals who made up the Harlem Renaissance, they too looked wistfully toward the African past. But other Negro leaders and the rank-and-file continued to be convinced, as in the days of their opposition to the Colonization Society, that their fate was bound up with ultimate integration into the American scene. Even black segregationism in a nationalist mold seemed abhorrent to those who could claim American ancestry since the seventeenth century. However, Garveyism never died despite its failures and the deportation of its leader; the movement had an estimated 7,000 members when Elijah Muhammed proclaimed the Black Muslim program.

The Great Depression bore down with the most force upon men and women who were the last hired and the first fired; but their resentments seemed appeased by the economic program of the New Deal, which converted Negro politicians and voters from their traditional allegiance to the party of Abraham Lincoln to the Democratic Party. However, there were intellectuals like Richard Wright (as a selection illustrates) who joined the Communists. Although Roosevelt had no specific racial program, his welfare benefits and minimum wage and hour guarantees and the efforts to enforce these meant a great deal to those at the bottom of the ladder.

The Negro participated vigorously in World War II—a war that seemed directed against racism. Once more, as war industries provided more and more job opportunities, a vast trek of Negroes moved northward and westward. In 1940-1943, the Negro population in Los Angeles grew by 30 per cent, in Chicago by 20 per cent, and in Detroit—which experienced a major race riot—by 19 per cent. The black belt of southern industrial cities also expanded phenomenally. Thus, the Negro ghetto of Norfolk, Virginia doubled in size and that of Charleston grew by 39 per cent.

Racial barriers to wartime jobs broke down in the face of labor scarcity and effective Negro leadership like that noted in an essay in this volume by A. Philip Randolph, president of the successful Brotherhood of Sleeping Car Porters. President Roosevelt averted a threatened Negro march on Washington by issuing his noted executive order forbidding discrimination in war plants. This victory for militant mass action set an important precedent for the Negro Revolution of the Sixties. As significant, though it did not outlast the war, was the Fair Employment Practices Act, which offered a model for the host of state and city FEPC's that followed.

Unlike World War I, which hardly affected the traditional segregationist barriers in the armed forces, the Second World War witnessed major reductions in discrimination. The Army commissioned nearly 7,800 Negro officers and even the more rigid Navy administrators removed certain of the restrictions upon Negroes eligible for posts better than the menial ones they had always filled. On the battlefield, the Negro Ninety-Second Division distinguished itself for bravery. But Negroes were humiliated to learn that the Red Cross segregated the blood of Negro donors.

As trains and buses full of Negroes arrived in northern and far western cities, they found a new instrument of progress in the protected ballot, which gave them an increasing number of outspoken Negro councilmen or aldermen in formerly all-white city councils. While the average Negro did not exercise his suffrage as fully as his white neighbors, there were enough voters to join with socially conscious whites to secure more welfare laws, urban renewal projects, and better public housing.

Negro pressures now counted for much more than formerly, especially as the race gained a balance of power position in many cities, and even on the state and federal levels. President Truman, calling attention to the fact that racism in America was severely damaging the country's foreign policy and its image abroad, embarked upon a strong civil rights program. His executive order of July 26, 1948 specified "equality of treatment for all persons in the armed forces without regard to race, color, or national origin." Despite protests by some high-ranking generals, this order was quickly and scrupulously fulfilled and it resulted in a gratifying rise in troop morale during the Korean War. The President also banned segregation in federally supported schools, though his "new charter of human freedom" failed to win over enough congressmen to pass the desired FEPC, a federal antilynching law, or laws abolishing poll taxes, white primaries, and residential restrictions on race.

Most encouraging to Negroes—and a starting point for the mass movement for Negro rights of the Sixties—was Chief Justice Earl Warren's decision in *Brown* v. *The Board of Education of Topeka* (1954), which followed a series of liberal court decisions banning segregation in interstate transportation and in other areas. This decision overthrew the doctrine of separate and equal accommodations established in the Plessy case (1896). From this point on, the Fourteenth Amendment meant equal protection of the law socially as well as politically—and this interpretation could lead to legislation outlawing segregation in public schools, libraries, restaurants, and other public places. "To separate [children] from others of similar age and qualifications solely because of their race," declared Warren, "generates a feeling of inferiority as to their status in the community that may affect their hearts and minds in a way unlikely ever to be undone. . . . Separate educational facilities are inherently unequal."

The real battle against segregationists has yet to be won by the NAACP and its allies. In Arkansas, Governor Orval E. Faubus, hitherto considered a moderate, used his state's National Guard to keep nine Negro children from entering Little Rock's Central High School and thus encouraged segregationists to initiate violence. But a federal injunction, President Eisenhower's federalized Arkansas National Guard, and a thousand federal paratroopers restored order. Still, in 1961, as President Kennedy took office, only

6 per cent of southern Negroes were attending mixed classes. Virginia's "massive resistance" program even closed certain public schools altogether. The Deep South refused to budge on the issue except to allow a few instances of token school integration.

In 1957 President Eisenhower succeeded in winning the first federal civil rights law since 1875. This law set up a Commission on Civil Rights to investigate racial discriminations; and penalities were prescribed for those intimidating voters. Eisenhower also appointed a Committee on Government Contracts. Federal courts intervened impressively again and again to reverse discriminatory southern court decisions as well as official actions to retard integration.

Negroes, encouraged by the progress made, especially by the favorable attitude of Presidents Eisenhower and Kennedy, but fearful that legal victories might degenerate into mere "tokenism," intensified their program of action. This new phase, called the "Negro Revolution," is usually dated from Martin Luther King's bus boycott of 1955. Not only the NAACP but also newer and more militant agencies like the Congress of Racial Equality (CORE) competed for Negro leadership. Almost every Negro intellectual of note participated in this nonviolent protest movement of the Negro Revolution. Perhaps the first national leader since Booker T. Washington was found in the Reverend Martin Luther King, Jr., whose career and ideas are examined in this anthology. His skillful use of the boycott began with the successful Montgomery, Alabama, public bus strike by Negro passengers. Freedom Riders tested the legality of the continued southern refusal to admit Negroes to public accommodations. Negro college students engaged in sit-ins and picketing against restaurants that did not serve Negroes. Old slogans of protest came back, such as "Don't Buy Where You Can't Work!" In the North, where Negroes were faced with considerable segregationism despite more liberal laws, New York Negroes first, followed by those in other large cities, urged that ghetto schools be abolished and Negro children redistributed to the less crowded white classrooms. The exclusivist policy of the unions, especially their rejection of Negro apprentices, was the object of determined biracial picketing. On August 27, 1963, 200,000 Negroes made a well-organized peaceful march on Washington to dramatize their demands.

Clergymen of both races and all major faiths cooperated in protesting racial discrimination. In Catholic Louisiana the Archbishop integrated parochial schools despite the racist protests of many of his communicants. Especially influential was the Kennedy antidiscrimination drive by all federal agencies, particularly through the Department of Justice under Attorney General Robert Kennedy. After President Kennedy's assassination his successor continued a vigorous drive to enact a national civil rights law.

A new variety of Garveyism arose in these years under Elijah Muhammed's Black Muslims, estimated to have perhaps 300,000 members (this number is probably exaggerated). As their official statement, reproduced in this anthology, shows, they stand for a black segregationism as absolute as the very opposite integrationist ideas of their civil rights opponents. From the gentle Booker T. Washington they took the idea of segregation, but they wanted it perpetual and militant. They also took Washington's emphasis upon the regeneration of the race through self-reliance, hard work, sobriety, cleanliness and skill; and they aimed to realize his hope for a Negro small-capitalist class, while adding some of the ideas for cooperatives held by Father Divine. But they angrily rejected the idea of racial accommodation that implied Negro subordination. Should the aspirations of the awakened urban Negro be frustrated, innumerable Negroes might find the Black Muslims acceptable. Meanwhile, the stepped-up demonstrations of the civil rights organizations raised warnings from Washington that violence threatened the cause of integration and civil rights.

Serious trials and tests obviously lay ahead. During the primary campaigns of 1964, Lily White Republicans, who as a group had never quarreled with racism, felt greatly encouraged by Senator Goldwater's popularity in most regions and by the fact that Governor Wallace of Alabama polled nearly a quarter of a million votes on a segregationist program in Wisconsin's primary and frightened Democratic regulars in the North by his strength in Maryland and elsewhere.

At the same time, integrationists took comfort in the weakening of age-old barriers in public accommodations, in the gains in suffrage and political power, in the advance of the Talented Tenth in professions and federal posts, and in the passage of the Twenty-Fourth Amendment to the Constitution outlawing the poll tax. And a new group of Negro leaders, better educated, more sophisticated and resourceful, and more determined than ever, had emerged.

Frederick Douglass

A giant literally and figuratively among militant Negro leaders was the ex-slave abolitionist and journalist Frederick Douglass (1817-1895). He was born at Tuckahoe, Talbot County, Maryland, of a slave mother with mixed Indian–Negro ancestry and of a white but unknown father. His highly literate *Autobiography* tells of a frustrated childhood, savage beatings, and resistance to his master (or mistress). He worked in relative freedom as a Baltimore house servant and managed in a very short time to learn to read and write. After being taken back as a field hand, he was jailed for trying to escape; he did succeed in running away to New York City on September 3, 1838. He married a free colored woman and worked for a time as a common laborer.

Garrison's *Liberator* fired him with enthusiasm for an active abolitionist career of organizing, speaking, and writing for the New England Anti-Slavery Society and for other reform groups. He fought the proslavery mobs, the prevailing Jim Crow practices of the North, and the efforts of Rhode Island to disfranchise Negroes. His enemies made it expedient for him to take a two-year trip to Great Britain and Ireland, where he was charmed by being treated as an equal and won converts to abolitionism.

For seventeen years, beginning in 1847, he edited an effective abolitionist weekly, *The North Star,* counseling shrewd practical tactics of liberation rather than outright violence. He aided the cause of women's suffrage and cooperated with Harriet Beecher Stowe in opening an industrial school for colored girls. When the Governor of Virginia sought to arrest him as a conspirator in John Brown's attack on Harper's Ferry he escaped to Canada.

During the Civil War he called upon Negro fighting men to join the two Massachusetts colored regiments, which included his own sons. He was one of the first to act as a national spokesman for his race, especially before President Lincoln. When the war ended, he became a Reconstruction leader—as the selection in this volume indicates, he urged Radical ideas for a prolonged northern domination; and he published the *National New Era,* which was dedicated to the freedmen, Negro suffrage, and civil rights, under the distressing circumstances that he describes in the *Autobiography*. In this same chapter he tells of his tragic involvement in the collapse of the "Freedmen's Bank," which he explained as a Benjamin Franklin type of capitalist experiment "to instill into the minds of the untutored Africans lessons of sobriety, wisdom, and economy, and to show how to rise in the world." This is certainly close, it would seem, to the middle-class philosophy of Booker T. Washington as expressed in *Up From Slavery*. The first selection is taken from *Life and Times of Frederick Douglass* (Boston: De Wolfe, Fish & Co., 1892), pp. 406-414.

The second selection, "Lynch Law in the South," appeared in *The North American Review,* CLV, No. 428 (1892), 17-24. Here Douglass analyzes the race issue realistically, calls for social equality, but also sternly warns southerners that they may drive the Negro to acts of desperation; at the same time he offers a keen explanation of the charges against the Negro.

I. Living and Learning

The adoption of the Fourteenth and Fifteenth Amendments and their incorporation into the Constitution of the United States opened a very tempting field to my ambition and one to which I should probably have yielded, had I been a younger man. I was earnestly urged by many of my respected fellow-citizens, both colored and white and from all sections of the country, to take up my abode in some one of the many districts of the South where there was a large colored vote, and get myself elected, as they were sure I easily could do, to a seat in Congress—possibly in the Senate. That I did not yield to this temptation was not entirely due to my age; for the idea did not square well with my better judgment and sense of propriety. The thought of going to live among a people in order to gain their votes and acquire official honors, was repugnant to my self-respect, and I had not lived long enough in the political atmosphere of Washington to have this sentiment sufficiently blunted to make me indifferent to its suggestions. I do not deny that the arguments of my friends had some weight in them, and from their standpoint it was all right; but I was better known to myself than to them. I had small faith in my aptitude as a politician, and could not hope to cope with rival aspirants. My life and labors in the North had in a measure unfitted me for such work, and I could not readily have adapted myself to the peculiar oratory found to be most effective with the newly enfranchised class. In the New England and northern atmosphere I had acquired a style of speaking which in the South would have been considered tame and spiritless; and, consequently, he who "could tear a passion to tatters and split the ear of groundlings," had far better chance of success with the masses there, than one so little boisterous as myself.

Upon the whole, I have never regretted that I did not enter the arena of Congressional honors to which I was invited.

Outside of mere personal considerations I saw, or thought I saw, that in the nature of the case the sceptre of power had passed from the old slave and rebellious states to the free and loyal states, and that hereafter, at least for some time to come, the loyal North, with its advanced civilization, must dictate the policy and control the destiny of the republic. I had an audience ready made in the free states; one which the labors of thirty years had prepared for me, and before this audience the freedmen of the South needed an advocate as much as they needed a member of Congress. I think in this I was right; for thus far our colored members of Congress have not largely made themselves felt in the legislation of the country; and I have little reason to think I could have done any better than they.

I was not, however, to remain long in my retired home in Rochester, where I had planted my trees and was reposing under their shadows. An effort was being made about this time to establish a large weekly newspaper in the city of Washington, which should be devoted to the defense and enlightenment of the newly emancipated and enfranchised people; and I was urged by such men as George T. Downing, J. H. Hawes, J. Sella Martin, and others, to become its editor-in-chief. My sixteen years' experience as editor and publisher of my own paper, and the knowledge of the toil and anxiety which such a relation to a public journal must impose, caused me much reluctance and hesitation: nevertheless, I yielded to the wishes of my friends and counselors, went to Washington, threw myself into the work, hoping to be able to lift up a standard at the national capital, for my people, which should cheer and strengthen them in the work of their own improvement and elevation.

I was not long connected with this enterprise, before I discovered my mistake. The cooperation so liberally promised, and the support which had been assured, were not very largely realized. By a series of circumstances a little bewildering as I now look back upon them, I found myself alone, under the mental and pecuniary burden involved in the prosecution of the enterprise. I had been misled by loud talk of a grand incorporated publishing company, in which I should have shares if I wished, and in any case a fixed salary for my services; and after all these fair-seeming conditions I had not been connected with the paper one year before its affairs had been so managed by the agent appointed by this invisible company or corporate body, as to compel me to bear the burden alone, and to become the sole owner of the printing establishment. Having become publicly associated with the enterprise, I was unwilling to have it prove a failure, and had allowed it to become in debt to me, both for money loaned, and for services, and at last it seemed wise that I should purchase the whole concern, which I did, and turned it over to my sons Lewis and Frederic, who were practical printers, and who, after a few years, were compelled to discontinue its publication. This paper was the *New National Era,* to the columns of which the colored people are indebted for some of the best things ever uttered in behalf of their cause; for, aside from its editorials and selections, many of the ablest colored men of the country made it the medium through which to convey their thoughts to the public. A misadventure though it was, which cost me from nine to ten thousand dollars, over it I have no tears to shed. The journal was valuable while it lasted, and the experiment was full of instruction to me, which has to some extent been heeded, for I have kept well out of newspaper undertakings since.

Someone has said that "experience is the best teacher." Unfortunately the wisdom acquired in one experience seems not to serve for another and new one; at any rate, my first lesson at the national capital, bought rather dearly as it was, did not preclude the necessity of a second whetstone to sharpen my wits in this my new home and new surroundings. It is not altogether without a feeling of humiliation that I must narrate my connection with the "Freedmen's Savings and Trust Company."

This was an institution designed to furnish a place of security and profit for the hard earnings of the colored people, especially in the South. Though its title was "The Freedmen's Savings and Trust Company," it is known generally as the "Freedmen's Bank." According to its managers it was to be this and something more. There was something missionary in its composition, and it dealt largely in exhortations as well as promises. The men connected with its management were generally church members, and reputed eminent for their piety. Some of its agents had been preachers of the "Word." Their aim was now to instill into the minds of the untutored Africans lessons of sobriety, wisdom, and economy, and to show them how to rise in the world. Circulars, tracts, and other papers were scattered like snowflakes in winter by this benevolent institution among the sable millions, and they were told to "look" to the Freedman's Bank and "live." Branches were established in all the southern states, and as a result, money flowed into its vaults to the amount of millions. With the usual effect of sudden wealth, the managers felt like making a little display of their prosperity. They accordingly erected one of the most costly and splendid buildings of the time on one of the most desirable and expensive sites in the national capital, finished on the inside with black walnut, and furnished with marble counters and all the modern improvements. The magnificent dimensions of the building bore testimony to its flourishing condition. In passing it on the street I often peeped into its spacious windows, and looked down the row of its gentlemanly and elegantly dressed colored clerks, with their pens behind their ears and button-hole bouquets in their coat-fronts, and felt my very eyes enriched. It was a sight I had never expected to see. I was amazed with the facility with which they counted the money; they threw off the thousands with the dexterity, if not the accuracy, of old and experienced clerks. The whole thing was beautiful. I had read of this bank when I lived in Rochester, and had indeed been solicited to become one of its trustees, and had reluctantly consented to do so; but when I came to Washington and saw its magnificent brown stone front, its towering height, and its perfect appointments, and the fine display it made in the transaction of its business, I felt like the Queen of Sheba when she saw the riches of Solomon, "the half had not been told me."

After settling myself down in Washington in the office of the *New Era,* I could and did occasionally attend the meetings of the board of trustees, and had the pleasure of listening to the rapid reports of the condition of the institution, which were generally of a most encouraging character. My confidence in the integrity and wisdom of the management was such that at one time I had entrusted to its vaults about twelve thousand dollars. It seemed fitting to me to cast in my lot with my brother freedmen, and help to build up an institution which represented their thrift and economy to so striking advantage; for the more millions accumulated there, I thought, the more consideration and respect would be shown to the colored people of the whole country.

About four months before this splendid institution was compelled to close its doors in the starved and deluded faces of its depositors, and while I was assured by its president and by its actuary of its sound condition, I was solicited by some of its trustees to allow them to use my name in the board as a candidate for its presidency. So I waked up one morning to find myself seated in a comfortable arm chair, with gold spectacles on my nose, and to hear myself addressed as president of the Freedmen's Bank. I could not help reflecting on the contrast between Frederick the slave boy, running about at Col. Lloyd's with only a tow linen shirt to cover him, and Frederick—president of a bank counting its assets by millions. I had heard of golden dreams, but such dreams had no comparison with this reality. And yet this seeming reality was scarcely more substantial than a dream. My term of service on this golden height covered only the brief space of three months, and these three months were divided into two parts, during the first part of which I was quietly employed in an effort to find out the real condition of the bank and its numerous branches. This was no easy task. On paper, and from the representations of its management, its assets amounted to three millions of dollars, and its liabilities were about equal to its assets. With such a showing I was encouraged in the belief that by curtailing expenses, doing away with nonpaying branches, which policy the trustees had now adopted, we could be carried safely through the financial distress then upon the country. So confident was I of this, that in order to meet what was said to be a temporary emergency, I was induced to loan the bank ten thousand dollars of my own money, to be held by it until it could realize on a part of its abundant securities. This money, though it was repaid, was not done so promptly as under the supposed circumstances I thought it should be, and these circumstances increased my fears lest the chasm was not so easily bridged as the actuary of the institution had assured me it could be. The more I observed and learned, the more my confidence diminished. I found that those trustees who wished to issue cards and publish addresses professing the utmost confidence in the bank, had themselves not one dollar deposited there. Some of them, while strongly assuring me of its soundness, had withdrawn their money and opened accounts elsewhere. Gradually I discovered that the bank had sustained heavy losses in the South through dishonest agents, that there was a discrepancy on the books of forty thousand dollars, for which no account could be given, that instead of our assets being equal to our liabilities we could not in all likelihood of the case pay seventy-two cents on the dollar. There was an air of mystery, too, about the spacious and elegant apartments of the bank building which greatly troubled me, and which I have only been able to explain to myself on the supposition that the employees, from the actuary and the inspector down to the messengers, were (perhaps) naturally anxious to hold their places, and consequently have the business continued. I am not a violent advocate of the doctrine of the total depravity of human nature. I am inclined, on the whole, to believe it a tolerably good nature, yet instances do occur which oblige me to concede that men can and do act from mere personal and selfish motives. In this case, at any rate, it seemed not unreasonable to conclude that the finely dressed young gentlemen, adorned with pens and bouquets, the most fashionable and genteel of all our colored youth, stationed behind those marble counters, should desire to retain their places as long as there was money in the vaults to pay them their salaries.

Standing on the platform of this large and complicated establishment, with its thirty-four branches, extending from New Orleans to Philadelphia, its machinery in full operation, its correspondence carried on in cipher, its actuary dashing in and out of the bank with an air of pressing business, if not of bewilderment, I found the path of enquiry I was pursuing an exceedingly difficult one. I knew there had been very lately several runs on the bank, and that there had been a heavy draft made upon its reserve fund, but I did not know what I should have been told before being allowed to enter upon the duties of my office, that this reserve, which the bank by its charter was required to keep, had been entirely exhausted, and that hence there was nothing left to meet any future emergency. Not to make too long a story, I was, in six weeks after my election as president of this bank, convinced that it was no longer a safe custodian of the hard earnings of my confiding people. This conclusion once reached, I could not hesitate as to my duty in the premises, and this was, to save as much as possible of the assets held by the bank for the benefit of the depositors; and to prevent their being further squandered in keeping up appearances, and in paying the salaries of myself and other officers in the bank. Fortunately, Congress, from which we held our charter, was then in session, and its committees on finance were in daily session. I felt it my duty to make known as speedily as possible to Hon. John Sherman, chairman of the Senate committee on finance, and to Senator Scott of Pennsylvania, also of the same committee, that I regarded the institution as insolvent and irrecoverable, and that I could no longer ask my people to deposit their money in it. This representation to the finance committee subjected me to very bitter opposition on the part of the officers of the bank. Its actuary, Mr. Stickney, immediately summoned some of the trustees, a dozen or so of them, to go before the finance committee and make a counter statement to that made by me; and this they did. Some of them who had assisted me by giving me facts showing the insolvency of the bank, now made haste to contradict that conclusion and to assure the committee that it was abundantly able to weather the financial storm, and pay dollar for dollar to its depositors if allowed to go on.

I was not exactly thunderstruck, but I was much amazed by this contradiction. I, however, adhered to my statement that the bank ought to stop. The finance committee substantially agreed with me, and in a few weeks so legislated as to bring this imposing banking business to a close by appointing three commissioners to take charge of its affairs.

This is a fair and unvarnished narration of my connection with the Freedmen's Savings and Trust Company, otherwise known as the Freedmen's Savings Bank, a connection which has brought upon my head an amount of abuse and detraction greater than any encountered in any other part of my life.

Before leaving the subject I ought in justice to myself state that when I found that the affairs of the bank were to be closed up, I did not, as I might easily have done, and as others did, make myself a preferred creditor and take my money out of the bank, but on the contrary, I determined to take my chances with other depositors, and left my money, to the amount of two thousand dollars, to be divided with the assets among the creditors of the bank. And now, after seven years have been allowed for the value of the securities to appreciate and the loss of interests on the deposits for that length of time, the depositors may deem themselves fortunate if they receive sixty cents on the dollar of what they placed in the care of this fine savings institution.

It is also due to myself to state, especially since I have seen myself accused of bringing the Freedmen's Bank into ruin, and squandering in senseless loans on bad security the hardly earned monies of my race, that all the loans ever made by the bank were made prior to my connection with it as its president. Not a dollar, not a dime of its millions were loaned by me, or with my approval. The fact is, and all investigation shows it, that I was married to a corpse. The fine building was there with its marble counters and black walnut finishings, the affable and agile clerks, and the discreet and comely colored cashier; but the LIFE, which was the money, was gone, and I found that I had been placed there with the hope that by "some drugs, some charms, some conjuration, or some mighty magic," I would bring it back.

When I became connected with the bank I had a tolerably fair name for honest dealing; I had expended in the publication of my paper in Rochester thousands of dollars annually, and had often to depend upon my credit to bridge over immediate wants, but no man there or elsewhere can say I ever wronged him out of a cent; and I could, today, with the confidence of the converted centurion, offer "to restore fourfold to any from whom I have unjustly taken aught." I say this, not for the benefit of those who know me, but for the thousands of my own race who hear of me mostly through the malicious and envious assaults of unscrupulous aspirants who vainly fancy that they left themselves into consideration by wanton attacks upon the characters of men who receive a larger share of respect and esteem than themselves.

II. Lynch Law in the South

The frequent and increasing resort to lynch law in our southern states, in dealing with alleged offenses by Negroes, marked as it is by features of cruelty which might well shock the sensibility of the most benighted savage, will not fail to attract the attention and animadversion of visitors to the World's Columbian Exposition.

Think of an American woman, in this year of grace 1892, mingling with a howling mob, and with her own hand applying the torch to the fagots around the body of a Negro condemned to death without a trial, and without judge or jury, as was done only a few weeks ago in the so-called civilized state of Arkansas.

When all lawful remedies for the prevention of crime have been employed and have failed; when criminals administer the law in the interest of crime; when the government has become a foul and damning conspiracy against the welfare of society; when men guilty of the most infamous crimes are permitted to escape with impunity; when there is no longer any reasonable ground upon which to base a hope of reformation, there is at least an apology for the application of lynch law; but, even in this extremity, it must be regarded as an effort to neutralize one poison by the employment of another. Certain it is that in no tolerable condition of society can lynch law be excused or defended. Its presence is either an evidence of governmental depravity, or of a demoralized state of society. It is generally in the hands of the worst class of men in the community, and is enacted under the most degrading and blinding influences. To break down the doors of jails, wrench off the iron bars of the cells, and in the dark hours of midnight drag out alleged criminals, and to shoot, hang, or burn them to death, requires preparation imparted by copious draughts of whiskey, which leave the actors without inclination or ability to judge of the guilt or innocence of the victims of their wrath.

The consensus of opinion in the early days of California permitted a vigilance committee, composed of respectable men, to hang a lot of thieves, thugs, gamblers and cut-throats; but it may now be fairly doubted whether even this example has not been an injury rather than a benefit to society, since it has been made the excuse for other uprisings of the people where there was no such justification as existed in California. But, granting that there may be instances where a sudden and spontaneous uprising of the populace may properly set aside the ordinary processes of the law for the punishment of crime and the preservation of society, it must still be admitted that there is, in the nature of the act itself, the essence of a crime more far-reaching, dangerous, and deadly than the crime it is intended to punish. Lynch law violates all of those merciful maxims of law and order which experience has shown to be wise and necessary for the protection of liberty, the security of the citizen, and the maintenance of justice for the whole people. It violates the principle which requires, for the conviction of crime, that a man shall be confronted in open court by his accusers. It violates the principle that it is better that ten guilty men shall escape than that one innocent man shall be punished. It violates the rule that presumes innocence until guilt is proven. It compels the accused to prove his innocence and denies him a reasonable doubt in his favor. It simply constitutes itself not a court of trial, but a court of execution. It comes to its work in a storm of passion and thirsting for human blood, ready to shoot, stab, or burn its victim, who is denied a word of entreaty or explanation. Like the gods of the heathen these mobs have eyes, but see not, ears, but hear not, and they rush to their work of death as pitilessly as the tiger rushes upon his prey.

Some of us are old enough to remember the storm of displeasure that came up from all the regions of slavery against William H.

Seward for the utterance of an idea of a higher law than the law of slavery. Then the South stood up stoutly for the authority and binding force of the regularly enacted laws, including even the infamous Fugitive Slave Law. It took to itself credit for being the conservative element in our government, but today it is the bold defender of the usurpations of the mob, and its territory, in many parts, has become the theater of lawless violence against a defenseless people. In the arguments in its defense, however, there is quite observable a slight degree of respect for the opinion of mankind and a disposition to conciliate that opinion. The crime which these usurpers of courts, laws, and juries profess to punish is the most revolting and shocking of any this side of murder. This they know is their best excuse, and it appeals at once and promptly to a prejudice which prevails in the North as well as the South. Hence we have for any act of lawless violence the same excuse, an outrage by a Negro upon some white woman. It is a notable fact, also, that it is not with them the immorality or the enormity of the crime itself that arouses popular wrath, but the emphasis is put upon the race and color of the parties to it. Here, and not there, is the ground of indignation and abhorrence. The appeal is not to the moral sense, but to the well-known hatred of one class toward another. It is an appeal that not only stops the ears and darkens the minds of southern men, but it palliates the crime of lawless violence in the eyes of northern men. The device is used with skill and effect, and the question of guilt or innocence becomes unimportant in the fierce tumult of popular passion.

For two hundred years or more, white men have in the South committed this offense against black women, and the fact has excited little attention, even in the North, except among abolitionists; which circumstance demonstrates that the horror now excited is not for the crime itself, but that it is based upon the reversal of colors in the participants. Yet this apology, rightly considered, utterly fails to palliate the crime of lynch law. For if the charge against the Negro is true, with the evidence of his guilt overwhelming, as is usually asserted, there could be no rational doubt of his certain punishment by the ordinary processes of the law. Thus the very argument in defense of the mob proves the criminality of the mob. If in any case there could be shown an element of doubt of the certain lawful conviction and punishment of the accused, there might be admitted some excuse for this lawless method of administering justice. But for no such doubt is there any contention. No decent white man in the South will pretend that in that region there could be impaneled a jury, black, white, or mixed, which would in case of proof of the deed allow a guilty Negro to escape condign punishment.

Whatever may be said of their weakness when required to hold a white man or a rich man, the meshes of the law are certainly always strong enough to hold and punish a poor man or a Negro. In this case there is neither color to blind, money to corrupt, nor powerful friends to influence court or jury against the claims of justice. All the presumptions of law and society are against the Negro. In the days of slavery he was presumed to be a slave, even if free, and his word was never taken against that of a white man. To be accused was to be condemned, and the same spirit prevails today. This state of opinion in the South not only assures by law the punishment of black men, but enables white men to escape punishment by assuming the color of the Negro in order to commit crime. It is often asserted that all Negroes look alike, and it is only necessary to bring one of the class into the presence of an accuser to have him at once identified as the criminal.

In apologizing for lynch law, Bishop Fitzgerald, of the Methodist Church South, says that the crime alleged against the Negro makes him an outlaw, and he goes on to complain of the North that it does not more fully sympathize with the South in its efforts to protect the purity of southern women. The answer to the first proposition of the learned and pious bishop is that no man is an outlaw unless declared to be such by some competent authority. It is not left to a lawless mob to determine whether a man is inside or outside the protection of the law. It is not for a dozen men or for a hundred men, constituting themselves a mob, to say whether or not Bishop Fitzgerald is an outlaw. We have courts, juries, and governors to determine that question, and it is a shame to the South that it holds in its bosom a bishop of the Church of Christ who could thus apologize for the subversion of all law. As to the sympathy of the North, there never was a time when it was more fully with the southern people than now.

The distressing circumstance in this revival of lynch law in different parts of the South is that it shows that prejudice and hatred have increased in bitterness with the increasing interval between the time of slavery and now. I have been frequently asked to explain this phase of our national problem. I explain it on the same principle by which resistance to the course of a ship is created and increased in proportion to her speed. The resistance met by the Negro is to me evidence that he is making progress. The Jew is hated in Russia, because he is thrifty. The Chinaman is hated in California because he is industrious and successful. The Negro meets no resistance when on a downward course. It is only when he rises in wealth, intelligence, and manly character that he brings upon himself the heavy hand of persecution. The men lynched at Memphis were murdered because they were prosperous. They were doing a business which a white firm desired to do,—hence the mob and hence the murder. When the Negro is degraded and ignorant he conforms to a popular standard of what a Negro should be. When he shakes off his rags and wretchedness and presumes to be a man, and a man among men, he contradicts this popular standard and becomes an offense to his surroundings. He can, in the South, ride in a first-class car as a servant, as an appendage to a white man, but is not allowed to ride in his quality of manhood alone. So extreme is the bitterness of this prejudice that several states have passed laws making it a crime for a conductor to allow a colored man, however respectable, to ride in the same car with white men unless in the manner above stated.

To the question, What is to be the solution of this race hatred and persecution? I have two answers, one of hope and one of fear. There may come in the South satiety even in the appetite for blood. When a wall is raised to a height inconsistent with the law of gravitation, it will fall. The South is not all a wilderness. There are good men and good women there who will sooner or later make themselves heard and felt. No people can long endure the shame and disgrace of lynch law. The South, which has been compelled to keep step with the music of the Union, will also be compelled to keep step with the music of the nineteenth century, which is pre-eminently a century of enlightenment and progress. The grand moral forces of this century no barbarism can withstand. They met serfdom in Russia, and it fell before them. They will meet our barbarism against color, and *it* will fall before them. I am the more encouraged in this belief because, in various parts of the North, and especially in the State of Massachusetts, where fifty years ago there existed the same proscription which at the present time prevails in the South, all men are now treated as equals before the law and are accorded the same civil rights.

I, however, freely confess that the present prospect has for me a gloomy side. When men sow the wind it is rational to expect that they will reap the whirlwind. It is evident to my mind that the Negro will not always rest a passive subject to the violence and bloodshed by which he is now pursued. If neither law nor public sentiment shall come to his relief, he will devise methods of his own. It should be remembered that the Negro is a man, and that in point of intelligence he is not what he was a hundred years ago. Whatever may be said of his failure to acquire wealth, it cannot be denied that he has made decided progress in the acquisition of knowledge; and he is a poor student of the natural history of civilization who does not see that the mental energies of this race, newly awakened and set in motion, must continue to advance. Character, with its moral influence; knowledge, with its power; and wealth, with its respectability, are possible to it as well as to other races of men. In arguing upon what will be the action of the Negro in case he continues to be the victim of lynch law I accept the statement often made in his disparagement, that he is an imitative being; that he will do what he sees other men do. He has already shown this facility, and he illustrates it all the way from the prize ring to the pulpit; from the plow to the professor's chair. The voice of nature, not less than the Book of books, teaches us that oppression can make even a wise man mad, and in such case the responsibility for madness will not rest upon the man but upon the oppression to which he is subjected.

How can the South hope to teach the Negro the sacredness of human life while it cheapens it and profanes it by the atrocities of mob law? The stream cannot rise higher than its source. The morality of the Negro will reach no higher point than the morality and religion that surround him. He reads of what is being done in the world in resentment of oppression and needs no teacher to make him understand what he reads. In warning the South that it may place too much reliance upon the cowardice of the Negro, I am not advocating violence by the Negro, but pointing out the dangerous tendency of his constant persecution. The Negro was not a coward at Bunker Hill; he was not a coward in Haiti; he was not a coward in the late war for the Union; he was not a coward at Harper's Ferry, with John Brown; and care should be taken against goading him to acts of desperation by continuing to punish him for heinous crimes of which he is not legally convicted.

I do not deny that the Negro may, in some instances, be guilty of the peculiar crime so often imputed to him. There are bad men among them, as there are bad men among all other varieties of the human family, but I contend that there is a good reason to question these lynch-law reports on this point. The crime imputed to the Negro is one most easily imputed and most difficult to disprove, and yet it is one that the Negro is least likely to commit. It is a crime for the commission of which opportunity is required, and no more convenient one was ever offered to any class of persons than was possessed by the Negroes of the South during the War of the Rebellion.

There were then left in their custody and in their power the wives and the daughters, the mothers and the sisters of the rebels, and during all that period no instance can be cited of an outrage committed by a Negro upon the person of any white woman. The crime is a new one for the Negro, so new that a doubt may be reasonably entertained that he has learned it to any such extent as his accusers would have us believe. A nation is not born in a day. It is said that the leopard cannot change his spots nor the Ethiopian his skin, and it may be as truly said that the character of a people, established by long years of consistent life and testimony, cannot be very suddenly reversed. It is improbable that this peaceful and inoffensive class has suddenly and all at once become changed into a class of the most daring and repulsive criminals.

Now, where rests the responsibility for the lynch law prevalent in the South? It is evident that it is not entirely with the ignorant mob. The men who break open jails and with bloody hands destroy human life are not alone responsible. These are not the men who make public sentiment. They are simply the hangmen, not the court, judge, or jury. They simply obey the public sentiment of the South, the sentiment created by wealth and respectability, by the press and the pulpit. A change in public sentiment can be easily effected by these forces whenever they shall elect to make the effort. Let the press and the pulpit of the South unite their power against the cruelty, disgrace, and shame that is settling like a mantle of fire upon these lynch-law states, and lynch law itself will soon cease to exist.

Nor is the South alone responsible for this burning shame and menace to our free institutions. Wherever contempt of race prevails, whether against African, Indian, or Mongolian, countenance and support are given to the present peculiar treatment of the Negro in the South. The finger of scorn in the North is correlated to the dagger of the assassin in the South. The sin against the Negro is both sectional and national, and until the voice of the North shall be heard in emphatic condemnation and withering reproach against these continued ruthless mob-law murders, it will remain equally involved with the South in this common crime.

Booker T. Washington

Like Frederick Douglass, Booker T. Washington (1856-1915) was born a plantation slave, of a Negro mother and probably a white father. In a shabby cabin in Franklin County, Virginia, the family eked out a living, but moved after emancipation to a village near Charleston, West Virginia, where Washington worked in a salt furnace and studied at night. The turning point in his life came when, at seventeen, he entered nearby Hampton Institute, aided by a white philanthropist. He earned his board as a janitor, learned the trade of brickmason, and was deeply influenced by the habits of neatness and order which he took as symbols of the truly emancipated Negro. After impressing the principal, General Samuel C. Armstrong, as a teacher and a secretary, he was invited in 1881 to head the projected Tuskegee Institute, sponsored by both races.

At Tuskegee he labored for thirty-four years with nationally recognized success and transformed a backward Negro community subsisting mainly on fat pork and corn bread to a progressive modern town respected by white Alabamans. He sent out thousands of trained teachers, craftsmen, and businessmen to numerous rural Negro villages, always emphasizing his own version of "learning by doing," rather than reliance on borrowed abstruse theories.

Unlike Douglass, he rejected militant racial tactics as dangerous in the tense South of the 1890's and the turn of the century in favor of conservative methods, although he hoped ultimately to win the same equalitarian objectives. As the following selection from his best known book, *Up From Slavery* shows, he stressed jobs first for the Negro, hoping that his race would become so indispensable economically that American society would open its doors to his people. In his famous Atlanta Exposition Address of 1895, delivered the year of Douglass' death, he reassured listening Georgians, "In all things that are purely social we can be as separate as the fingers, yet one as the hand in all things essential to mutual progress." He pointed out the Negro's loyalty, his immunity to unions and strikes, and his conviction that social agitation was the "extremest folly." "The opportunity to earn a dollar in a factory just now is worth infinitely more than the opportunity to spend a dollar in an opera house," he said. His insistence on the importance of industrial education was not unique among Americans of that day, nor actually disputed even by Du Bois, but liberals feared that Washington ignored the Talented Tenth and left the Negro forever as a hewer of wood and a drawer of water. He seemed to speak for the entire race, supported as he was by rich philanthropists who backed Negro welfare, by powerful industrialists who profited by Negro strikebreakers and open shop adherents, and even by southern legislatures, who felt that he was "safe." While Du Bois moved ever leftward, Washington hoped to create a large class of Negro businessmen and substantial farmowners—the mirage of a "black bourgeoisie" that has been riddled by the late Dr. E. Franklin Frazier.

Militants doubted from the beginning whether Washington knew the solution to the growing race crisis after 1885, with its lynchings, disfranchisement, and newly legalized Jim Crow. Expediency, tact, and bargaining with merchant princes—the Washington Way—did not seem heroic. Some intellectuals even blamed the Tuskegee leader for the period's outbreaks of racial violence. Yet Washington worked behind the scenes against disfranchisement and brutality and found funds to fight for Negro rights; however, he stubbornly avoided any confrontation with the southern white. He urged Negroes to vote Democratic like their southern white neighbors, but to save their Republican votes for national issues. It is noteworthy that the founders of the NAACP did not include Tuskegee's head.

The two selections below are from Booker T. Washington's *Up From Slavery* (Boston: Houghton, Mifflin, 1901), pp. 80-91, 217-237. Often overlooked are his demands for equal suffrage, his conviction that mass education was as important as jobs, and his belief that the conservative philosophy of the Atlanta Exposition Address was a temporary expedient based on the assumption that the Negro would always live in the South and that eventual economic stabilization would lead the South to rectify racial injustices.

I. The Reconstruction Period

The years from 1867 to 1878 I think may be called the period of Reconstruction. This included the time that I spent as a student at Hampton and as a teacher in West Virginia. During the whole of the Reconstruction period two ideas were constantly agitating the minds of the colored people, or, at least, the minds of a large part of the race. One of these was the craze for Greek and Latin learning, and the other was a desire to hold office.

It could not have been expected that a people who had spent generations in slavery, and before that, generations in the darkest heathenism, could at first form any proper conception of what an education meant. In every part of the South, during the Reconstruction period, schools, both day and night, were filled to overflowing with people of all ages and conditions, some being as far along in age as sixty and seventy years. The ambition to secure an education was most praiseworthy and encouraging. The idea, however, was too prevalent that, as soon as one secured a little education, in some unexplainable way he would be free from most of the hardships of the world, and, at any rate, could live without manual labor. There was a further feeling that a knowledge, however little, of the Greek and Latin languages would make one a very superior human being, something bordering almost on the supernatural. I remember that the first colored man whom I saw who knew something about foreign languages impressed me at that time as being a man of all others to be envied.

Naturally, most of our people who received some little education became teachers or preachers. While among these two classes there were many capable, earnest, godly men and women, still a large proportion took up teaching or preaching as an easy way to make a living. Many became teachers who could do little more than write their names. I remember there came into our neighborhood one of this class, who was in search of a school to teach, and the question arose while he was there as to the shape of the earth and how he would teach the children concerning this subject. He explained his position in the matter by saying that he was prepared to teach that the earth was either flat or round, according to the preference of a majority of his patrons.

The ministry was the profession that suffered most—and still suffers, though there has been great improvement—on account of not only ignorant but in many cases immoral men who claimed that they were "called to preach." In the earlier days of freedom almost every colored man who learned to read would receive "a call to preach" within a few days after he began reading. At my home in West Virginia the process of being called to the ministry was a very interesting one. Usually the "call" came when the individual was sitting in church. Without warning the one called would fall upon the floor as if struck by a bullet, and would lie there for hours, speechless and motionless. Then the news would spread all through the neighborhood that this individual had received a "call." If he were inclined to resist the summons, he would fall or be made to fall a second or third time. In the end he always yielded to the call. While I wanted an education badly, I confess that in my youth I had a fear that when I had learned to read and write well I would receive one of these "calls"; but, for some reason, my call never came.

When we add the number of wholly ignorant men who preached or "exhorted" to that of those who possessed something of an education, it can be seen at a glance that the supply of ministers was large. In fact, some time ago I knew a certain church that had a total membership of about two hundred, and eighteen of that number were ministers. But, I repeat, in many communities in the South the character of the ministry is being improved, and I believe that within the next two or three decades a very large proportion of the unworthy ones will have disappeared. The "calls" to preach, I am glad to say, are not nearly so numerous now as they were formerly, and the calls to some industrial occupation are growing more numerous. The improvement that has taken place in the character of the teachers is even more marked than in the case of the ministers.

During the whole of the Reconstruction period our people throughout the South looked to the federal government for everything, very much as a child looks to its mother. This was not unnatural. The central government gave them freedom, and the whole nation had been enriched for more than two centuries by the labor of the Negro. Even as a youth, and later in manhood, I had the feeling that it was cruelly wrong in the central government, at the beginning of our freedom, to fail to make some provision for the general education of our people in addition to what the states might do, so that the people would be the better prepared for the duties of citizenship.

It is easy to find fault, to remark what might have been done, and perhaps, after all, and under all the circumstances, those in charge of the conduct of affairs did the only thing that could be done at the time. Still, as I look back now over the entire period of our freedom, I cannot help feeling that it would have been wiser if some plan could have been put in operation which would have made the possession of a certain amount of education or property, or both, a test for the exercise of the franchise, and a way provided by which this test should be made to apply honestly and squarely to both the white and black races.

Though I was but little more than a youth during the period of Reconstruction, I had the feeling that mistakes were being made, and that things could not remain in the condition that they were in then very long. I felt that the Reconstruction policy, so far as it related to my race, was in a large measure on a false foundation, was artificial and forced. In many cases it seemed to me that the ignorance of my race was being used as a tool with which to help white men into office, and that there was an element in the North which wanted to punish the southern white men by forcing the Negro into positions over the heads of the southern whites. I felt that the Negro would be the one to suffer for this in the end. Besides, the general political agitation drew the attention of our people away from the more fundamental matters of perfecting themselves in the industries at their doors and in securing property.

The temptations to enter political life were so alluring that I came very near yielding to them at one time, but I was kept from doing so by the feeling that I would be helping in a more substantial way by assisting in the laying of the foundation of the race through a generous education of the hand, head, and heart. I saw colored men who were members of the state legislatures, and county officers, who, in some cases, could not read or write, and whose morals were as weak as their education. Not long ago, when passing through the streets of a certain city in the South, I heard some brickmasons calling out, from the top of a two-story brick building on which they were working, for the "Governor" to "hurry up and bring up some more bricks." Several times I heard the command, "Hurry up, Governor!" "Hurry up, Governor!" My curiosity was aroused to such an extent that I made inquiry as to who the "Governor" was, and soon found that he was a colored man who at one time had held the position of lieutenant-governor of his state.

But not all the colored people who were in office during Reconstruction were unworthy of their positions, by any means. Some of them, like the late Senator B. K. Bruce, Governor Pinchback, and many others, were strong, upright, useful men. Neither were all the class designated as carpetbaggers dishonorable men. Some of them, like ex-Governor Bullock, of Georgia, were men of high character and usefulness.

Of course the colored people, so largely without education, and wholly without experience in government, made tremendous mistakes, just as any people similarly situated would have done. Many of the southern whites have a feeling that, if the Negro is permitted to exercise his political rights now to any degree, the mistakes of the Reconstruction period will repeat themselves. I do not think this would be true, because the Negro is a much stronger and wiser man than he was thirty-five years ago, and he is fast learning the lesson that he cannot afford to act in a manner that will alienate his southern white neighbors from him. More and more I am convinced that the final solution of the political end of our race problem will be for each state that finds it necessary to change the law bearing upon the franchise to make the law apply with absolute honesty, and without opportunity for double dealing or evasion, to both races alike. Any other course, my daily observation in the South convinces me, will be unjust to the Negro, unjust to the white man, and unfair to the rest of the states in the Union, and will be, like slavery, a sin that at some time we shall have to pay for.

In the fall of 1878, after having taught school in Malden for two years, and after I had succeeded in preparing several of the young men and women, besides my two brothers, to enter the Hampton Institute, I decided to spend some months in study at Washington, D.C. I remained there for eight months. I derived a great deal of benefit from the studies which I pursued, and I came into contact with some strong men and women. At the institution I attended there was no industrial training given to the students, and I had an opportunity of comparing the influence of an institution with no industrial training with that of one like the Hampton Institute, that emphasized the industries. At this school I found the students, in most cases, had more money, were better dressed, wore the latest style of all manner of clothing, and in some cases were more brilliant mentally. At Hampton it was a standing rule that, while the institution would be responsible for securing someone to pay the tuition for the students, the men and women themselves must provide for their own board, books, clothing, and room wholly by work, or partly by work and partly in cash. At the institution at which I now was, I found that a large proportion of the students by some means had their personal expenses paid for them. At Hampton the student was constantly making the effort through the industries to help himself, and that very effort was of immense value in character-building. The students at the other school seemed to be less self-dependent. They seemed to give more attention to mere outward appearances. In a word, they did not appear to me to be beginning at the bottom, on a real, solid foundation, to the extent that they were at Hampton. They knew more about Latin and Greek when they left school, but they seemed to know less about life and its conditions as they would meet it in their homes. Having lived for a number of years in the midst of comfortable surroundings, they were not as much inclined as the Hampton students to go into the country districts of the South, where there was little of comfort, to take up work for our people, and they were more inclined to yield to the temptation to become hotel waiters and Pullman-car porters as their life-work.

During the time I was a student in Washington the city was crowded with colored people, many of whom had recently come from the South. A large proportion of these people had been drawn to Washington because they felt that they could lead a life of ease there. Others had secured minor government positions, and still another large class was there in the hope of securing federal positions. A number of colored men—some of them very strong and brilliant—were in the House of Representatives at that time, and one, the Hon. B. K. Bruce, was in the Senate. All this tended to make Washington an attractive place for members of the colored race. Then, too, they knew that at all times they could have the protection of the law in the District of Columbia. The public schools in Washington for colored people were better then than they were elsewhere. I took great interest in studying the life of our people there closely at that time. I found that while among them there was a large element of substantial, worthy citizens, there was also a superficiality about the life of a large class that greatly alarmed me. I saw young colored men who were not earning more than four dollars a week spend two dollars or more for a buggy on Sunday to ride up and down Pennsylvania Avenue in, in order that they might try to convince the world that they were worth thousands. I saw other young men who received seventy-five or one hundred dollars per month from the government, who were in debt at the end of every month. I saw men who but a few months previous were members of Congress, then without employment and in poverty. Among a large class there seemed to be a dependence upon the government for every conceivable thing. The members of this class had little ambition to create a position for themselves, but wanted the federal officials to create one for them. How many times I wished then, and have often wished since, that by some power of magic I might remove the great bulk of these people into the country districts and plant them upon the soil, upon the solid and never deceptive foundation of Mother Nature, where all nations and races that have ever succeeded have gotten their start,—a start that at first may be slow and toilsome, but one that nevertheless is real.

In Washington I saw girls whose mothers were earning their living by laundrying. These girls were taught by their mothers, in rather a crude way it is true, the industry of laundrying. Later, these girls entered the public schools and remained there perhaps six or eight years. When the public-school course was finally finished, they wanted more costly dresses, more costly hats and shoes. In a word, while their wants had been increased, their ability to supply their wants had not been increased in the same degree. On the other hand, their six or eight years of book education had weaned them away from the occupation of their fathers. The result of this was in too many cases that the girls went to the bad. I often thought how much wiser it would have been to give these girls the same amount of mental training—and I favor any kind of training, whether in the languages or mathematics, that gives strength and culture to the mind—but at the same time to give them the most thorough training in the latest and best methods of laundrying and other kindred occupations.

II. The Atlanta Exposition Address

The Atlanta Exposition, at which I had been asked to make an address as a representative of the Negro race, was opened with a short address from Governor Bullock. After other interesting exercises, including an invocation from Bishop Nelson, of Georgia, a dedicatory ode by Albert Howell, Jr., and addresses by the President of the Exposition and Mrs. Joseph Thompson, the president of the Woman's Board, Governor Bullock introduced me with the words, "We have with us today a representative of Negro enterprise and Negro civilization."

When I arose to speak, there was considerable cheering, especially from the colored people. As I remember it now, the thing that was uppermost in my mind was the desire to say something that would cement the friendship of the races and bring about hearty cooperation between them. So far as my outward surroundings were concerned, the only thing that I recall distinctly now is that when I got up, I saw thousands of eyes looking intently into my face. The following is the address which I delivered:

Mr. President and Gentlemen of the Board
of Directors and Citizens:

One-third of the population of the South is of the Negro race. No enterprise seeking the material, civil, or moral welfare of this section can disregard this element of our population and reach the highest success. I but convey to you, Mr. President and Directors, the sentiment of the masses of my race when I say that in no way have the value and manhood of the American Negro been more fittingly and generously recognized than by the managers of this magnificent exposition at every stage of its progress. It is a recognition that will do more to cement the friendship of the two races than any occurrence since the dawn of our freedom.

Not only this, but the opportunity here afforded will awaken among us a new era of industrial progress. Ignorant and inexperienced, it is not strange that in the first years of our new life we began at the top instead of at the bottom; that a seat in Congress or the state legislature was more sought than real estate or industrial skill; that the political convention or stump speaking had more attractions than starting a dairy farm or truck garden.

A ship lost at sea for many days suddenly sighted a friendly vessel. From the mast of the unfortunate vessel was seen a signal, "Water, water; we die of thirst!" The answer from the friendly vessel at once came back, "Cast down your bucket where you are." A second time the signal, "Water, water; send us water!" ran up from the distressed vessel, and was answered, "Cast down your bucket where you are." And a third and fourth signal for water was answered, "Cast down your bucket where you are." The captain of the distressed vessel, at last heeding the injunction, cast down his bucket, and it came up full of fresh, sparkling water from the mouth of the Amazon River. To those of my race who depend on bettering their condition in a foreign land or who underestimate the importance of cultivating friendly relations with the southern white man, who is their next-door neighbor, I would say: "Cast down your bucket where you are"—cast it down in making friends in every manly way of the people of all races by whom we are surrounded.

Cast it down in agriculture, mechanics, in commerce, in domestic service, and in the professions. And in this connection it is well to bear in mind that whatever other sins the South may be called to bear, when it comes to business, pure and simple, it is in the South that the Negro is given a man's chance in the commercial world, and in nothing is this exposition more eloquent than in emphasizing this chance. Our greatest danger is that in the great leap from slavery to freedom we may overlook the fact that the masses of us are to live by the productions of our hands, and fail to keep in mind that we shall prosper in proportion as we learn to dignify and glorify common labor and put brains and skill into the common occupations of life; shall prosper in proportion as we learn to draw the line between the superficial and the substantial, the ornamental gewgaws of life and the useful. No race can prosper till it learns that there is as much dignity in tilling a field as in writing a poem. It is at the bottom of life we must begin, and not at the top. Nor should we permit our grievances to overshadow our opportunities.

To those of the white race who look to the incoming of those of foreign birth and strange tongue and habits for the prosperity of the South, were I permitted I would repeat what I say to my own race, "Cast down your bucket where you are." Cast it down among the eight millions of Negroes whose habits you know, whose fidelity and love you have tested in days when to have proved treacherous meant the ruin of your firesides. Cast down your bucket among these people who have, without strikes and labor wars, tilled your fields, cleared your forests, builded your railroads and cities, and brought forth treasures from the bowels of the earth, and helped make possible this magnificent representation of the progress of the South. Casting down your bucket among my people, helping and encouraging them as you are doing on these grounds, and to education of head, hand, and heart, you will find that they will buy your surplus land, make blossom the waste places in your fields, and run your factories. While doing this, you can be sure in the future, as in the past, that you and your families will be surrounded by the most patient, faithful, law-abiding, and unresentful people that the world has seen. As we have proved our loyalty to you in the past, in nursing your children, watching by the sick-bed of your mothers and fathers, and often following them with tear-dimmed eyes to their graves, so in the future, in our humble way, we shall stand by you with a devotion that no foreigner can approach, ready to lay down our lives, if need be, in defense of yours, interlacing our industrial, commercial, civil, and religious life with yours in a way that shall make the interests of both races one. In all things that are purely social we can be as separate as the fingers, yet one as the hand in all things essential to mutual progress.

There is no defense or security for any of us except in the highest intelligence and development of all. If anywhere there are efforts tending to curtail the fullest growth of the Negro, let these efforts be turned into stimulating, encouraging, and making him the most useful and intelligent citizen. Effort or means so invested will pay a thousand per cent interest. These efforts will be twice blessed—"blessing him that gives and him that takes."

There is no escape through law of man or God from the inevitable:—

The laws of changeless justice bind
Oppressor with oppressed;

And close as sin and suffering joined
We march to fate abreast.

Nearly sixteen millions of hands will aid you in pulling the load upward, or they will pull against you the load downward. We shall constitute one-third and more of the ignorance and crime of the South, or one-third its intelligence and progress; we shall contribute one-third to the business and industrial prosperity of the South, or we shall prove a veritable body of death, stagnating, depressing, retarding every effort to advance the body politic.

Gentlemen of the Exposition, as we present to you our humble effort at an exhibition of our progress, you must not expect overmuch. Starting thirty years ago with ownership here and there in a few quilts and pumpkins and chickens (gathered from miscellaneous sources), remember the path that has led from these to the inventions and production of agricultural implements, buggies, steam-engines, newspapers, books, statuary, carving, paintings, the management of drugstores and banks, has not been trodden without contact with thorns and thistles. While we take pride in what we exhibit as a result of our independent efforts, we do not for a moment forget that our part in this exhibition would fall far short of your expectations but for the constant help that has come to our educational life, not only from the southern states, but especially from northern philanthropists, who have made their gifts a constant stream of blessing and encouragement.

The wisest among my race understand that the agitation of questions of social equality is the extremest folly, and that progress in the enjoyment of all the privileges that will come to us must be the result of severe and constant struggle rather than of artificial forcing. No race that has anything to contribute to the markets of the world is long in any degree ostracized. It is important and right that all privileges of the law be ours, but it is vastly more important that we be prepared for the exercises of these privileges. The opportunity to earn a dollar in a factory just now is worth infinitely more than the opportunity to spend a dollar in an opera house.

In conclusion, may I repeat that nothing in thirty years has given us more hope and encouragement and drawn us so near to you of the white race, as this opportunity offered by the exposition; and here bending, as it were, over the altar that represents the results of the struggles of your race and mine, both starting practically empty-handed three decades ago, I pledge that in your effort to work out the great and intricate problem which God has laid at the doors of the South, you shall have at all times the patient, sympathetic help of my race. Only let this be constantly in mind: that, while from representations in these buildings of the product of field, of forest, of mine, of factory, letters, and art much good will come, yet far above and beyond ma-

> terial benefits will be that higher good, that, let us pray God, will come, in a blotting out of sectional differences and racial animosities and suspicions, in a determination to administer absolute justice, in a willing obedience among all classes to the mandates of law. This, coupled with our material prosperity, will bring into our beloved South a new heaven and a new earth.

The first thing that I remember, after I had finished speaking, was that Governor Bullock rushed across the platform and took me by the hand, and that others did the same. I received so many and such hearty congratulations that I found it difficult to get out of the building. I did not appreciate to any degree, however, the impression which my address seemed to have made, until the next morning, when I went into the business part of the city. As soon as I was recognized, I was surprised to find myself pointed out and surrounded by a crowd of men who wished to shake hands with me. This was kept up on every street on to which I went, to an extent which embarrassed me so much that I went back to my boarding-place. The next morning I returned to Tuskegee. At the station in Atlanta, and at almost all of the stations at which the train stopped between that city and Tuskegee, I found a crowd of people anxious to shake hands with me.

The papers in all parts of the United States published the address in full, and for months afterward there were complimentary editorial references to it. Mr. Clark Howell, the editor of the Atlanta *Constitution,* telegraphed to a New York paper, among other words, the following, "I do not exaggerate when I say that Professor Booker T. Washington's address yesterday was one of the most notable speeches, both as to character and as to the warmth of its reception, ever delivered to a southern audience. The address was a revelation. The whole speech is a platform upon which blacks and whites can stand with full justice to each other."

The Boston *Transcript* said editorially: "The speech of Booker T. Washington at the Atlanta Exposition, this week, seems to have dwarfed all the other proceedings and the exposition itself. The sensation that it has caused in the press has never been equalled."

I very soon began receiving all kinds of propositions from lecture bureaus, and editors of magazines and papers, to take the lecture platform, and to write articles. One lecture bureau offered me fifteen thousand dollars, or two hundred dollars a night and expenses, if I would place my services at his disposal for a given period. To all these communications I replied that my life-work was at Tuskegee; and that whenever I spoke it must be in the interests of the Tuskegee school and my race and that I would enter into no arrangements that seemed to place a mere commercial value upon my services.

Some days after its delivery I sent a copy of my address to the President of the United States, the Hon. Grover Cleveland. I received from him the following autograph reply:

GRAY GABLES, BUZZARD'S BAY, MASS.
October 6, 1895

BOOKER T. WASHINGTON, ESQ.:

MY DEAR SIR: I thank you for sending me a copy of your address delivered at the Atlanta Exposition.

I thank you with much enthusiasm for making the address. I have read it with intense interest, and I think the Exposition would be fully justified if it did not do more than furnish the opportunity for its delivery. Your words cannot fail to delight and encourage all who wish well for your race; and if our colored fellow-citizens do not from your utterances gather new hope and form new determinations to gain every valuable advantage offered them by their citizenship, it will be strange indeed.

Yours very truly,
GROVER CLEVELAND

. . . The colored people and the colored newspapers at first seemed to be greatly pleased with the character of my Atlanta address, as well as with its reception. But after the first burst of enthusiasm began to die away, and the colored people began reading the speech in cold type, some of them seemed to feel that they had been hypnotized. They seemed to feel that I had been too liberal in my remarks toward the southern whites, and that I had not spoken out strongly enough for what they termed the "rights" of the race. For a while there was a reaction, so far as a certain element of my own race was concerned, but later these reactionary ones seemed to have been won over to my way of believing and acting.

While speaking of changes in public sentiment, I recall that about ten years after the school at Tuskegee was established, I had an experience that I shall never forget. Dr. Lyman Abbott, then the pastor of Plymouth Church, and also editor of the *Outlook* (then the *Christian Union*), asked me to write a letter for his paper giving my opinion of the exact condition, mental and moral, of the colored ministers in the South, as based upon my observations. I wrote the letter, giving the exact facts as I conceived them to be. The picture painted was a rather black one—or, since I am black, shall I say "white"? It could not be otherwise with a race but a few years out of slavery, a race which had not had time or opportunity to produce a competent ministry.

What I said soon reached every Negro minister in the country, I think, and the letters of condemnation which I received from them were not few. I think that for a year after the publication of this article every association and every conference or religious body of any kind, of my race, that met, did not fail before adjourning to pass a resolution condemning me, or calling upon me to retract or modify what I had said. Many of these organizations went so far in their resolutions as to advise parents to cease sending their children to Tuskegee. One association even appointed a "missionary" whose duty it was to warn the people against sending their children to Tuskegee. This missionary had a son in the school, and I noticed that, whatever the "missionary" might have said or done with regard to others, he was careful not to take his son away from the institution. Many of the colored papers, especially those that were the organs of religious bodies, joined in the general chorus of condemnation or demands for retraction.

During the whole time of the excitement, and through all the criticism, I did not utter a word of explanation or retraction. I knew that I was right, and that time and the sober second thought of the people would vindicate me. It was not long before the bishops and other church leaders began to make a careful investigation of the conditions of the ministry, and they found out that I was right. In fact, the oldest and most influential bishop in one branch of the Methodist Church said that my words were far too mild. Very soon public sentiment began making itself felt, in demanding a purifying of the ministry. While this is not yet complete by any means, I think I may say, without egotism, and I have been told by many of our most influential ministers, that my words had much to do with starting a demand for the placing of a higher type of men in the pulpit. I have had the satisfaction of having many who once condemned me thank me heartily for my frank words.

The change of the attitude of the Negro ministry, so far as regards myself, is so complete that at the present time I have no warmer friends among any class than I have among the clergymen. The improvement in the character and life of the Negro ministers is one of the most gratifying evidences of the progress of the race. My experience with them, as well as other events in my life, convince me that the thing to do, when one feels sure that he has said or done the right thing, and is condemned, is to stand still and keep quiet. If he is right, time will show it. . . .

I am often asked to express myself more freely than I do upon the political condition and the political future of my race. These recollections of my experience in Atlanta give me the opportunity to do so briefly. My own belief is, although I have never before said so in so many words, that the time will come when the Negro in the South will be accorded all the political rights which his ability, character, and material possessions entitle him to. I think, though, that the opportunity to freely exercise such political rights will not come in any large degree through outside or artificial forcing, but will be accorded to the Negro by the southern white people themselves, and that they will protect him in the exercise of those rights. Just as soon as the South gets over the old feeling that it is being forced by "foreigners," or "aliens," to do something which it does not want to do, I believe that the change in the direction that I have indicated is going to begin. In fact, there are indications that it is already beginning in a slight degree.

Let me illustrate my meaning. Suppose that some months before the opening of the Atlanta Exposition there had been a general demand from the press and public platform outside the South that a Negro be given a place on the opening program, and that a Negro be placed upon the board of jurors of award. Would any such recognition of the race have taken place? I do not think so. The Atlanta officials went as far as they did because they felt it to be a pleasure, as well as a duty, to reward what they considered merit in the Negro race. Say what we will, there is something in human nature which we cannot blot out, which makes one man, in the end, recognize and reward merit in another, regardless of color or race.

I believe it is the duty of the Negro—as the greater part of the race is already doing—to deport himself modestly in regard to political claims, depending upon the slow but sure influences that proceed from the possession of property, intelligence, and high character for the full recognition of his political rights. I think that the according of the full exercise of political rights is going to be a matter of natural, slow growth, not an over-night, gourd-vine affair. I do not believe that the Negro should cease voting, for a man cannot learn the exercise of self-government by ceasing to vote, any more than a boy can learn to swim by keeping out of the water, but I do believe that in his voting he should more and more be influenced by those of intelligence and character who are his next-door neighbors.

I know colored men who, through the encouragement, help, and advice of southern white people, have accumulated thousands of dollars' worth of property, but who, at the same time, would never think of going to those same persons for advice concerning the casting of their ballots. This, it seems to me, is unwise and unreasonable, and should cease. In saying this I do not mean that the Negro should truckle, or not vote from principle, for the instant he ceases to vote from principle he loses the confidence and respect of the southern white man even.

I do not believe that any state should make a law that permits an ignorant and poverty-stricken white man to vote, and prevents a black man in the same condition from voting. Such a law is not only unjust, but it will react, as all unjust laws do, in time; for the effect of such a law is to encourage the Negro to secure education and property, and at the same time it encourages the white man to remain in ignorance and poverty. I believe that in time, through the operation of intelligence and friendly race relations, all cheating at the ballot-box in the South will cease. It will become apparent that the white man who begins by cheating a Negro out of his ballot soon learns to cheat a white man out of his, and that the man who does this ends his career of dishonesty by the theft of property or by some equally serious crime. In my opinion, the time will come when the South will encourage all of its citizens to vote. It will see that it pays better, from every standpoint, to have healthy, vigorous life than to have that political stagnation which always results when one-half of the population has no share and no interest in the government.

As a rule, I believe in universal, free suffrage, but I believe that in the South we are confronted with peculiar conditions that justify the protection of the ballot in many of the states, for a while at least, either by an educational test, a property test, or by both combined; but whatever tests are required, they should be made to apply with equal and exact justice to both races.

William E. B. Du Bois

Dr. Du Bois (1868-1963), the third major race leader, clearly belonged to the militant tradition of Douglass despite great differences in personality, for he was reserved in manner, handsomely impressive with his Vandyke beard and cane, and rather proud of his mixed ancestry and New England background. A Negro leader of racially mixed ancestry was not as apt to propose a purely racial solution to the Negro's problems as are some of the African leaders of the 1960's. Du Bois was born in Great Barrington, Massachusetts, on February 23, 1868, and his early aptitudes and sponsors secured him many educational opportunities. He took an A.B. at Fisk University, Tennessee, where he also encountered Jim Crow for the first time; his M.A. and Ph.D. came from Harvard. Aided by the Slater Fund, he studied at the University of Berlin, where a Negro was somewhat of an anomaly. His thesis, *The Suppression of the African Slave Trade,* charged with some exaggeration that southern slaveowners had conspired with federal officials to evade the strict laws against African slave importations up to the Civil War.

He taught Greek and Latin at Wilberforce in 1894-1896—in fact he almost accepted Booker T. Washington's personal invitation to come to Tuskegee, but the offer came too late. As an assistant at the University of Pennsylvania, he published his shrewd sociological observations in *The Philadelphia Negro* (1899). From 1896 to 1910 he was professor of history and economics at the popular Negro institution Atlanta University, which many budding racial leaders attended, and was the moving spirit and editor behind the remarkable Atlanta Conferences which produced annual studies on Negro problems of unusual depth and militancy. In one of these studies, he tries to demonstrate that school funds were being diverted from Negro to white institutions and that the Negro taxpayer actually paid for all of the education for his race and for that of many white children as well.

After many years of temporizing with the ideas of the Atlanta Compromise of 1895, he suddenly broke with Booker T. Washington in his

The Souls of Black Folk, a brilliant, sensitively written series of acid-tipped essays on Negro questions. At the same time he was writing numerous essays and articles in national as well as local journals.

In 1905 he brought together militant young Negroes, mostly professional men, in the Niagara Movement and wrote its bold manifesto calling for the abolition of all racial restrictions in suffrage, civil rights, jobs, welfare provisions, and educational opportunities. "We will not be satisfied to take one jot or tittle less than our full manhood rights . . . and until we get these rights we will never cease to protest and assail the ears of America."

Four years later he became the chief Negro leader in the newly formed biracial NAACP and editor of *The Crisis;* he remained at this task of publicity for twenty-four years. Well-photographed lynchings and other atrocities appeared in the pages of his publication. During World War I, he turned to a favorite idea of the unity of all colored peoples everywhere, particularly favoring a kind of Pan-Africanism. While Marcus Garvey called for a grass-roots back-to-Africa movement for the masses, Du Bois organized a Pan-African Congress in 1919 in Paris, but failed to ignite any spark for a united Africa.

Du Bois is credited with writing nineteen books, including a life of John Brown and a radical Marxist interpretation, *Black Reconstruction* (1935), which pointed out the positive educational and welfare achievements of the much-depreciated carpetbag legislatures. A trip to the Soviet Union had hastened his conversion to Marxist ideas, but he conceded himself a Communist only after his ninetieth year. Meanwhile he stimulated many contemporary-minded historical studies by editing the new socially conscious *Phylon Quarterly Review.* He died in Ghana in 1963, a guest of Nkrumah, having shortly before become a citizen of that nation.

The first selection below, "Of Booker T. Washington and Others," is from Du Bois's *The Souls of Black Folk* (Chicago: A. C. McClurg, 1903), pp. 41-59. The final paragraph, it will be noted, shows that Du Bois still agreed with the Washington emphasis on thrift, patience, and industrial education, but utterly rejected what he considered to be apologies for injustice, racial disfranchisement, and the neglect of higher education for the Talented Tenth—his favorite phrase—although he did not wish special privileges for an educated elite. The second selection, "The Talented Tenth," is from *The Negro Problem* (New York: James Pott, 1903), pp. 31-75.

I. Of Mr. Booker T. Washington and Others

Easily the most striking thing in the history of the American Negro since 1876 is the ascendancy of Mr. Booker T. Washington. It began at the time when war memories and ideals were rapidly passing; a day of astonishing commercial development was dawning; a sense of doubts and hesitation overtook the freedmen's sons, —then it was that his leading began. Mr. Washington came, with a simple definite program, at the psychological moment when the nation was a little ashamed of having bestowed so much sentiment on Negroes, and was concentrating its energies on Dollars. His program of industrial education, conciliation of the South, and submission and silence as to civil and political rights, was not wholly original; the free Negroes from 1830 up to wartime had striven to build industrial schools, and the American Missionary Association had from the first taught various trades; and Price and others had sought a way of honorable alliance with the best of the southerners. But Mr. Washington first indissolubly linked these things; he put enthusiasm, unlimited energy, and perfect faith into this program, and changed it from a by-path into a veritable Way of Life. And the tale of the methods by which he did this is a fascinating study of human life.

It startled the nation to hear a Negro advocating such a program after many decades of bitter complaint; it startled and won the applause of the South, it interested and won the admiration of the North; and after a confused murmur of protest, it silenced if it did not convert the Negroes themselves.

To gain the sympathy and cooperation of the various elements comprising the white South was Mr. Washington's first task; and this, at the time Tuskegee was founded, seemed, for a black man, well-nigh impossible. And yet ten years later it was done in the word spoken at Atlanta: "In all things purely social we can be as separate as the five fingers, and yet one as the hand in all things essential to mutual progress." This "Atlanta Compromise" is by all odds the most notable thing in Mr. Washington's career. The South interpreted it in different ways: the Radicals received it as a complete surrender of the demand for civil and political equality; the conservatives, as a generously conceived working basis for mutual understanding. So both approved it, and today its author is certainly the most distinguished southerner since Jefferson Davis, and the one with the largest personal following.

Next to this achievement comes Mr. Washington's work in gaining place and consideration in the North. Others less shrewd and tactful had formerly essayed to sit on these two stools and had fallen between them; but as Mr. Washington knew the heart of the South from birth and training, so by singular insight he intuitively grasped the spirit of the age which was dominating the North. And so thoroughly did he learn the speech and thought of triumphant commercialism, and the ideals of material prosperity, that the picture of a lone black boy poring over a French grammar amid the weeds and dirt of a neglected home soon seemed to him the acme of absurdities. One wonders what Socrates and St. Francis of Assisi would say to this.

And yet this very singleness of vision and thorough oneness with his age is a mark of the successful man. It is as though Nature must needs make men narrow in order to give them force. So Mr. Washington's cult has gained unquestioning followers, his work has wonderfully prospered, his friends are legion, and his enemies are confounded. Today he stands as the one recognized spokesman of his ten million fellows, and one of the most notable figures in a nation of seventy millions. One hesitates, therefore, to criticize a life which, beginning with so little, has done so much. And yet the time is come when one may speak in all sincerity and utter courtesy of the mistakes and shortcomings of Mr. Washington's career, as well as of his triumphs, without being thought captious or envious, and without forgetting that it is easier to do ill than well in the world.

The criticism that has hitherto met Mr. Washington has not always been of this broad character. In the South especially has he had to walk warily to avoid the harshest judgments,—and naturally so, for he is dealing with the one subject of deepest sensitiveness to that section. Twice—once when at the Chicago celebration of the Spanish American War he alluded to the color-prejudice that was "eating away the vitals of the South," and once when he dined with President Roosevelt—has the resulting southern criticism been violent enough to threaten seriously his popularity. In the North the feeling has several times forced itself into words, that Mr. Washington's counsels of submission overlooked certain elements of true manhood, and that his educational program was unnecessarily narrow. Usually, however, such criticism has not found open expression, although, too, the spiritual sons of the Abolitionists have not been prepared to acknowledge that the schools founded before Tuskegee, by men of broad ideals and self-sacrificing spirit, were wholly failures or worthy of ridicule. While, then, criticism has not failed to follow Mr. Washington, yet the prevailing public opinion of the land has been but too willing to deliver the solution of a wearisome problem into his hands, and say, "If that is all you and your race ask, take it."

Among his own people, however, Mr. Washington has encountered the strongest and most lasting opposition, amounting at times to bitterness, and even today continuing strong and insistent even though largely silenced in outward expression by the public opinion of the nation. Some of this opposition is, of course, mere envy; the disappointment of displaced demagogues and the spite of narrow minds. But aside from this, there is among educated and thoughtful colored men in all parts of the land a feeling of deep regret, sorrow, and apprehension at the wide currency and ascendancy which some of Mr. Washington's theories have gained. These same men admire his sincerity of purpose, and are willing to forgive much to honest endeavor which is doing something worth the doing. They cooperate with Mr. Washington as far as they conscientiously can; and, indeed, it is no ordinary tribute to this man's tact and power that, steering as he must between so many diverse interests and opinions, he so largely retains the respect of all.

But the hushing of the criticism of honest opponents is a dangerous thing. It leads some of the best of the critics to unfortunate silence and paralysis of effort, and others to burst into speech so passionately and intemperately as to lose listeners. Honest and earnest criticism from those whose interests are most nearly touched, —criticism of writers by readers, of government by those governed, of leaders by those led,—this is the soul of democracy and the safeguard of modern society. If the best of the American Negroes receive by outer pressure a leader whom they had not recognized before, manifestly there is here a certain palpable gain. Yet there is also irreparable loss,—a loss of that peculiarly valuable education which a group receives when by search and criticism it finds and commissions its own leaders. The way in which this is done is at once the most elementary and the nicest problem of social growth. History is but the record of such group-leadership; and yet how infinitely changeful is its type and character! And of all types and kinds, what can be more instructive than the leadership of a group within a group?—that curious double movement where real progress may be negative and actual advance be relative retrogression. All this is the social student's inspiration and despair.

Now in the past the American Negro has had instructive experience in the choosing of group leaders, founding thus a peculiar dynasty which in the light of present conditions is worthwhile studying. When sticks and stones and beasts form the sole environment of a people, their attitude is largely one of determined opposition to and conquest of natural forces. But when to earth and brute is added an environment of men and ideas, then the attitude of the imprisoned group may take three main forms,—a feeling of revolt and revenge; an attempt to adjust all thought and action to the will of the greater group; or, finally, a determined effort at self-realization and self-development despite environing opinion. The influence of all of these attitudes at various times can be traced in the history of the American Negro, and in the evolution of his successive leaders.

Before 1750, while the fire of African freedom still burned in the veins of the slaves, there was in all leadership or attempted leadership but the one motive of revolt and revenge,—typified in the terrible Maroons, the Danish blacks, and Cato of Stono, and veiling all the Americas in fear of insurrection. The liberalizing tendencies of the latter half of the eighteenth century brought, along with kindlier relations between black and white, thoughts of ultimate adjustment and assimilation. Such aspiration was especially voiced in the earnest songs of Phyllis, in the martyrdom of Attucks, the fighting of Salem and Poor, the intellectual accomplishments of Banneker and Derham, and the political demands of the Cuffes.

Stern financial and social stress after the war cooled much of the previous humanitarian ardor. The disappointment and impatience of the Negroes at the persistence of slavery and serfdom voiced itself in two movements. The slaves in the South, aroused undoubtedly by vague rumors of the Haitian revolt, made three fierce attempts at insurrection,—in 1800 under Gabriel in Virginia, in 1822 under Vesey in Carolina, and in 1831 again in Virginia under the terrible Nat Turner. In the Free States, on the other hand, a new and curious attempt at self-development was made. In Philadelphia and New York color-proscription led to a withdrawal of Negro communicants from white churches and the formation of a peculiar socio-religious institution among the Negroes known as the African Church,—an organization still living and controlling in its various branches over a million men.

Walker's wild appeal against the trend of the times showed how the world was changing after the coming of the cotton-gin. By 1830 slavery seemed hopelessly fastened on the South, and the slaves thoroughly cowed into submission. The free Negroes of the North, inspired by the mulatto immigrants from the West Indies, began to change the basis of their demands; they recognized the slavery of slaves, but insisted that they themselves were freemen, and sought assimilation and amalgamation with the nation on the same terms with other men. Thus, Forten and Purvis of Philadelphia, Shad of Wilmington, Du Bois of New Haven, Barbadoes of Boston, and others, strove singly and together as men, they said, not as slaves; as "people of color," not as "Negroes." The trend of the times, however, refused them recognition save in individual and exceptional cases, considered them as one with all the despised blacks, and they soon found themselves striving to keep even the rights they formerly had of voting and working and moving as freemen. Schemes of migration and colonization arose among them; but these they refused to entertain, and they eventually turned to the Abolition movement as a final refuge.

Here, led by Remond, Nell, Wells-Brown, and Douglass, a new period of self-assertion and self-development dawned. To be sure, ultimate freedom and assimilation was the ideal before the leaders, but the assertion of the manhood rights of the Negro by himself was the main reliance, and John Brown's raid was the extreme of its logic. After the war and emancipation, the great form of Frederick Douglass, the greatest of American Negro leaders, still led the host. Self-assertion, especially in political lines, was the main program, and behind Douglass came Elliot, Bruce, and Langston, and the Reconstruction politicians, and, less conspicuous but of greater social significance Alexander Crummell and Bishop Daniel Payne.

Then came the Revolution of 1876, the suppression of the Negro votes, the changing and shifting of ideals, and the seeking of new lights in the great night. Douglass, in his old age, still bravely stood for the ideals of his early manhood,—ultimate assimilation *through* self-assertion, and on no other terms. For a time Price arose as a new leader, destined, it seemed, not to give up, but to restate the old ideals in a form less repugnant to the white South. But he passed away in his prime. Then came the new leader. Nearly all the former ones had become leaders by the silent suffrage of their fellows, had sought to lead their own people alone, and were usually, save Douglass, little known outside their race. But Booker T. Washington arose as essentially the leader not of one race but of two,—a compromiser between the South, the North, and the Negro. Naturally the Negroes resented, at first bitterly, signs of compromise which surrendered their civil and political rights, even though this was to be exchanged for larger chances of economic development. The rich and dominating North, however, was not only weary of the race problem, but was investing largely in southern enterprises, and welcomed any method of peaceful cooperation. Thus, by national opinion, the Negroes began to recognize Mr. Washington's leadership; and the voice of criticism was hushed.

Mr. Washington represents in Negro thought the old attitude of adjustment and submission; but adjustment at such a peculiar time as to make his program unique. This is an age of unusual economic development, and Mr. Washington's program naturally takes an economic cast, becoming a gospel of Work and Money to such an extent as apparently almost completely to overshadow the higher aims of life. Moreover, this is an age when the more advanced races are coming in closer contact with the less developed races, and the race-feeling is therefore intensified; and Mr. Washington's program practically accepts the alleged inferiority of the Negro races. Again, in our own land, the reaction from the sentiment of wartime has given impetus to race prejudice against Negroes, and Mr. Washington withdraws many of the high demands of Negroes as men and American citizens. In other periods of intensified prejudice all the Negro's tendency to self-assertion has been called forth; at this period a policy of submission is advocated. In the history of nearly all other races and peoples the doctrine preached at such crises has been that manly self-respect is worth more than lands and houses, and that a people who voluntarily surrender such respect, or cease striving for it, are not worth civilizing.

In answer to this, it has been claimed that the Negro can survive only through submission. Mr. Washington distinctly asks that black people give up, at least for the present, three things,—

First, political power,

Second, insistence on civil rights,

Third, higher education of Negro youth,—

and concentrate all their energies on industrial education, the accumulation of wealth, and the conciliation of the South. This policy has been courageously and insistently advocated for over fifteen years, and has been triumphant for perhaps ten years. As a result of this tender of the palm-branch, what has been the return? In these years there have occurred:

1. The disfranchisement of the Negro,
2. The legal creation of a distinct status of civil inferiority for the Negro,
3. The steady withdrawal of aid from institutions for the higher training of the Negro.

These movements are not, to be sure, direct results of Mr. Washington's teachings; but his propaganda has, without a shadow of doubt, helped their speedier accomplishment. The question then comes: Is it possible, and probable, that nine millions of men can make effective progress in economic lines if they are deprived of political rights, made a servile caste, and allowed only the most meagre chance for developing their exceptional men? If history and reason give any distinct answer to these questions, it is an emphatic *No.* And Mr. Washington thus faces the triple paradox of his career:

1. He is striving nobly to make Negro artisans, businessmen, and property-owners; but it is utterly impossible, under modern competitive methods, for workingmen and property-owners to defend their rights and exist without the right of suffrage.

2. He insists on thrift and self-respect, but at the same time counsels a silent submission to civic inferiority such as is bound to sap the manhood of any race in the long run.

3. He advocates common-school and industrial training, and depreciates institutions of higher learning; but neither the Negro common-schools, nor Tuskegee itself, could remain open a day were it not for teachers trained in Negro colleges, or trained by their graduates.

This triple paradox in Mr. Washington's position is the object of criticism by two classes of colored Americans. One class is spiritually descended from Toussaint the Savior, through Gabriel, Vesey, and Turner, and they represent the attitude of revolt and revenge; they hate the white South blindly and distrust the white race generally, and so far as they agree on definite action, think that the Negro's only hope lies in emigration beyond the borders of the United States. And yet, by the irony of fate, nothing has more effectually made this program seem hopeless than the recent course of the United States toward weaker and darker peoples in the West Indies, Hawaii, and the Philippines,—for where in the world may we go and be safe from lying and brute force?

The other class of Negroes who cannot agree with Mr. Washington has hitherto said little aloud. They deprecate the sight of scattered counsels, of internal disagreement; and especially they dislike making their just criticism of a useful and earnest man an excuse for a general discharge of venom from small-minded opponents. Nevertheless, the questions involved are so fundamental and serious that it is difficult to see how men like the Grimkes, Kelly Miller, J. W. E. Bowen, and other representatives of this group, can much longer be silent. Such men feel in conscience bound to ask of this nation three things:

1. The right to vote.
2. Civic equality.

3. The education of youth according to ability.

They acknowledge Mr. Washington's invaluable service in counseling patience and courtesy in such demands; they do not ask that ignorant black men vote when ignorant whites are debarred, or that any reasonable restrictions in the suffrage should not be applied; they know that the low social level of the mass of the race is responsible for much discrimination against it, but they also know, and the nation knows, that relentless color prejudice is more often a cause than a result of the Negro's degradation; they seek the abatement of this relic of barbarism, and not its systematic encouragement and pampering by all agencies of social power from the Associated Press to the Church of Christ. They advocate, with Mr. Washington, a broad system of Negro common schools supplemented by thorough industrial training; but they are surprised that a man of Mr. Washington's insight cannot see that no such educational system ever has rested or can rest on any other basis than that of the well-equipped college and university, and they insist that there is a demand for a few such institutions throughout the South to train the best of the Negro youth as teachers, professional men, and leaders.

This group of men honor Mr. Washington for his attitude of conciliation toward the white South; they accept the "Atlanta Compromise" in its broadest interpretation; they recognize, with him, many signs of promise, many men of high purpose and fair judgment, in this section; they know that no easy task has been laid upon a region already tottering under heavy burdens. But, nevertheless, they insist that the way to truth and right lies in straightforward honesty, not in indiscriminate flattery; in praising those of the South who do well and criticizing uncompromisingly those who do ill; in taking advantage of the opportunities at hand and urging their fellows to do the same, but at the same time in remembering that only a firm adherence to their higher ideals and aspirations will ever keep those ideals within the realm of possibility. They do not expect that the free right to vote, to enjoy civic rights, and to be educated, will come in a moment; they do not expect to see the bias and prejudices of years disappear at the blast of a trumpet; but they are absolutely certain that the way for a people to gain their reasonable rights is not by voluntarily throwing them away and insisting that they do not want them; that the way for a people to gain respect is not by continually belittling and ridiculing themselves; that, on the contrary, Negroes must insist continually, in season and out of season, that voting is necessary to modern manhood, that color discrimination is barbarism, and that black boys need education as well as white boys.

In failing thus to state plainly and unequivocally the legitimate demands of their people, even at the cost of opposing an honored leader, the thinking classes of American Negroes would shirk a heavy responsibility,—a responsibility to themselves, a responsibility to the struggling masses, a responsibility to the darker races of men whose future depends so largely on this American experiment, but especially a responsibility to this nation,—this common Fatherland. It is wrong to encourage a man or a people in evil-doing; it is wrong to aid and abet a national crime simply because it is unpopular not to do so. The growing spirit of kindliness and reconciliation between the North and South after the frightful differences of a generation ago ought to be a source of deep congratulation to all, and especially to those whose mistreatment caused the war; but if that reconciliation is to be marked by the industrial slavery and civic death of those same black men, with permanent legislation into a position of inferiority, then those black men, if they are really men, are called upon by every consideration of patriotism and loyalty to oppose such a course by all civilized methods, even though such opposition involves disagreement with Mr. Booker T. Washington. We have no right to sit silently by while the inevitable seeds are sown for a harvest of disaster to our children, black and white.

First, it is the duty of black men to judge the South discriminatingly. The present generation of southerners are not responsible for the past, and they should not be blindly hated or blamed for it. Furthermore, to no class is the indiscriminate endorsement of the recent course of the South toward Negroes more nauseating than to the best thought of the South. The South is not "solid"; it is a land in the ferment of social change, wherein forces of all kinds are fighting for supremacy; and to praise the ill the South is today perpetrating is just as wrong as to condemn the good. Discriminating and broad-minded criticism is what the South needs,—needs it for the sake of her own white sons and daughters, and for the insurance of robust, healthy mental and moral development.

Today even the attitude of the southern whites toward the blacks is not, as so many assume, in all cases the same; the ignorant southerner hates the Negro, the workingmen fear his competition, the money-makers wish to use him as a laborer, some of the educated see a menace in his upward development, while others—usually the sons of the masters—wish to help him to rise. National opinion has enabled this last class to maintain the Negro common schools, and to protect the Negro partially in property, life, and limb. Through the pressure of the money-makers, the Negro is in danger of being reduced to semi-slavery, especially in the country districts; the workingmen, and those of the educated who fear the Negro, have united to disfranchise him, and some have urged his deportation; while the passions of the ignorant are easily aroused to lynch and abuse any black man. To praise this intricate whirl of thought and prejudice is nonsense; to inveigh indiscriminately against "the South" is unjust; but to use the same breath in praising Governor Aycock, exposing Senator Morgan, arguing with Mr. Thomas Nelson Page, and denouncing Senator Ben Tillman, is not only sane, but the imperative duty of thinking black men.

It would be unjust to Mr. Washington not to acknowledge that in several instances he has opposed movements in the South which were unjust to the Negro; he sent memorials to the Louisiana and Alabama constitutional conventions, he has spoken against lynching, and in other ways has openly or silently set his influence against sinister schemes and unfortunate happenings. Notwithstanding this, it is equally true to assert that on the whole the distinct impression left by Mr. Washington's propaganda is, first, that the South is justified in its present attitude toward the Negro because of the Negro's degradation; secondly, that the prime cause of the Negro's failure to rise more quickly is his wrong education in the past; and, thirdly, that his future rise depends primarily on his own efforts. Each of these propositions is a dangerous half-truth. The supplementary truths must never be lost sight of: first, slavery and race prejudice are potent if not sufficient causes of the Negro's position; second, industrial and common-school training were necessarily slow in planting because they had to await the black teachers trained by higher institutions,—it being extremely doubtful if any essentially different development was possible, and certainly a Tuskegee was unthinkable before 1880; and, third, while it is a great truth to say that the Negro must strive and strive mightily to help himself, it is equally true that unless his striving be not simply seconded, but rather aroused and encouraged, by the initiative of the richer and wiser environing group, he cannot hope for great success.

In his failure to realize and impress this last point, Mr. Washington is especially to be criticized. His doctrine has tended to make the whites, North and South, shift the burden of the Negro problem to the Negro's shoulders and stand aside as critical and rather pessimistic spectators; when in fact the burden belongs to the nation, and the hands of none of us are clean if we bend not our energies to righting these great wrongs.

The South ought to be led, by candid and honest criticism, to assert her better self and do her full duty to the race she has cruelly wronged and is still wronging. The North—her co-partner in guilt—cannot salve her conscience by plastering it with gold. We cannot settle this problem by diplomacy and suaveness, by "policy" alone. If worse comes to worst, can the moral fibre of this country survive the slow throttling and murder of nine millions of men?

The black men of America have a duty to perform, a duty stern and delicate,—a forward movement to oppose a part of the work of their greatest leader. So far as Mr. Washington preaches Thrift, Patience, and Industrial Training for the masses, we must hold up his hands and strive with him, rejoicing in his honors and glorying in the strength of this Joshua called of God and of man to lead the headless host. But so far as Mr. Washington apologizes for injustice, North or South, does not rightly value the privilege and duty of voting, belittles the emasculating effects of caste distinctions, and opposes the higher training and ambition of our brighter minds,—so far as he, the South, or the Nation, does this,—we must unceasingly and firmly oppose them. By every civilized and peaceful method we must strive for the rights which the world accords to men, clinging unwaveringly to those great words which the sons of the Fathers would fain forget: "We hold these truths to be self-evident: That all men are created equal; that they are endowed by their Creator with certain unalienable rights; that among these are life, liberty, and the pursuit of happiness."

II. The Talented Tenth

The Negro race, like all races, is going to be saved by its exceptional men. The problem of education, then, among Negroes must first of all deal with the Talented Tenth; it is the problem of developing the Best of this race that they may guide the Mass away from the contamination and death of the Worst, in their own and other races. Now the training of men is a difficult and intricate task. Its technique is a matter for educational experts, but its object is for the vision of seers. If we make money the object of man-training, we shall develop money-makers but not necessarily men; if we make technical skill the object of education, we may possess artisans but not, in nature, men. Men we shall have only as we make manhood the object of the work of the schools—intelligence, broad sympathy, knowledge of the world that was and is, and of the relation of men to it—this is the curriculum of that Higher Education which must underlie true life. On this foundation we may build bread-winning skill of hand and quickness of brain, with never a fear lest the child and man mistake the means of living for the object of life. . . .

You misjudge us because you do not know us. From the very first it has been the educated and intelligent of the Negro people that have led and elevated the mass, and the sole obstacles that nullified and retarded their efforts were slavery and race prejudice; for what is slavery but the legalized survival of the unfit and the nullification of the work of natural internal leadership? Negro leadership, therefore, sought from the first to rid the race of this awful incubus that it might make way for natural selection and the survival of the fittest. In colonial days came Phillis Wheatley and Paul Cuffe striving against the bars of prejudice; and Benjamin Banneker, the almanac maker, voiced their longings. . . .

Where were these black abolitionists trained? Some, like Frederick Douglass, were self-trained, but yet trained liberally; others, like Alexander Crummell and McCune Smith, graduated from famous foreign universities. Most of them rose up through the colored schools of New York and Philadelphia and Boston, taught by college-bred men like Russworm, of Dartmouth, and college-bred white men like Neau and Benezet.

After emancipation came a new group of educated and gifted leaders: Langston, Bruce and Elliot, Greener, Williams and Payne. Through political organization, historical and polemic writing, and moral regeneration, these men strove to uplift their people. It is the fashion of today to sneer at them and to say that with freedom Negro leadership should have begun at the plow and not in the Senate—a foolish and mischievous lie; two hundred and fifty years that black serf toiled at the plow and yet that toiling was in vain till the Senate passed the war amendments; and two hundred and fifty years more the half-free serf of today may toil at his plow, but unless he have political rights and righteously guarded civic status, he will still remain the poverty-stricken and ignorant plaything of rascals, that he now is. This all sane men know even if they dare not say it.

And so we come to the present—a day of cowardice and vacillation, of strident wide-voiced wrong and faint-hearted compromise; of double-faced dallying with Truth and Right. Who are today guiding the work of the Negro people? The "exceptions" of course. And yet so sure as this Talented Tenth is pointed out, the blind worshippers of the Average cry out in alarm: "These are exceptions, look here at death, disease and crime—these are the happy rule." Of course they are the rule, because a silly nation made them the rule: Because for three long centuries this people lynched Negroes who dared to be brave, raped black women who dared to be virtuous, crushed dark-hued youth who dared to be ambitious, and encouraged and made to flourish servility and lewdness and apathy. But not even this was able to crush all manhood and chastity and aspiration from black folk. A saving remnant continually survives and persists, continually aspires, continually shows itself in thrift and ability and character. Exceptional it is to be sure, but this is its chiefest promise; it shows the capability of Negro blood, the promise of black men. Do Americans ever stop to reflect that there are in this land a million men of Negro blood, well-educated, owners of homes, against the honor of whose womanhood no breath was ever raised, whose men occupy positions of trust and usefulness, and who, judged by any standard, have reached the full measure of the best type of modern European culture? Is it fair, is it decent, is it Christian to ignore these facts of the Negro problem, to belittle such aspiration, to nullify such leadership and seek to crush these people back into the mass out of which by toil and travail, they and their fathers have raised themselves? . . .

How then shall the leaders of a struggling people be trained and the hands of the risen few strengthened? There can be but one answer: The best and most capable of their youth must be schooled in the colleges and universities of the land. We will not quarrel as to just what the university of the Negro should teach or how it should teach it—I willingly admit that each soul and each race-soul needs its own peculiar curriculum. But this is true: A university is a human invention for the transmission of knowledge and culture from generation to generation, through the training of quick minds and pure hearts, and for this work no other human invention will suffice, not even trade and industrial schools.

All men cannot go to college but some men must; every isolated group or nation must have its yeast, must have for the talented few centers of training where men are not so mystified and befuddled by the hard and necessary toil of earning a living, as to have no aims higher than their bellies, and no God greater than Gold. This is true training, and thus in the beginning were the favored sons of the freedmen trained. . . . Where ought they to have begun to build? At the bottom, of course, quibbles the mole with his eyes in the earth. Aye! truly at the bottom, at the very bottom; at the bottom of knowledge, down in the very depths of knowledge there where the roots of justice strike into the lowest soil of Truth. And so they did begin; they founded colleges, and up from the colleges shot normal schools, and out from the normal schools went teachers, and around the normal teachers clustered other teachers to teach the public schools; the college trained in Greek and Latin and mathematics, 2,000 men; and these men trained full 50,000 others in morals and manners, and they in turn taught thrift and the alphabet to nine millions of men, who today hold $300,000,000 of property. It was a miracle—the most wonderful peace-battle of the nineteenth century, and yet today men smile at it, and in fine superiority tell us that it was all a strange mistake; that a proper way to found a system of education is first to gather the children and buy them spelling books and hoes; afterward men may look about for teachers, if haply they may find them; or again they would teach men Work, but as for Life—why, what has Work to do with Life, they ask vacantly.

Was the work of these college founders successful; did it stand the test of time? Did the college graduates, with all their fine theories of life, really live? Are they useful men helping to civilize and elevate their less fortunate fellows? Let us see. Omitting all institutions which have not actually graduated students from a college course, there are today in the United States thirty-four institutions giving something above high school training to Negroes and designed especially for this race.

Three of these were established in border states before the war; thirteen were planted by the Freedmen's Bureau in the years 1864-1869; nine were established between 1870 and 1880 by various church bodies; five were established after 1881 by Negro churches, and four are state institutions supported by United States agricultural funds. In most cases the college departments are small adjuncts to high- and common-school work. As a matter of fact six institutions—Atlanta, Fisk, Howard, Shaw, Wilberforce, and Leland, are the important Negro colleges so far as actual work and number of students are concerned. In all these institutions, seven hundred and fifty Negro college students are enrolled. In grade the best of these colleges are about a year behind the smaller New England colleges and a typical curriculum is that of Atlanta University. Here students from the grammar grades, after a three years' high-school course, take a college course of 136 weeks. One-fourth of this time is given to Latin and Greek; one-fifth, to English and modern languages; one-sixth, to history and social science; one-seventh, to natural science; one-eighth to mathematics, and one-eighth to philosophy and pedagogy.

In addition to these students in the South, Negroes have attended Northern colleges for many years. As early as 1826 one was graduated from Bowdoin College, and from that time till today nearly every year has seen elsewhere other such graduates. They have, of course, met much color prejudice. Fifty years ago very few colleges would admit them at all. Even today no Negro has ever been admitted to Princeton, and at some other leading institutions they are rather endured than encouraged. Oberlin was the great pioneer in the work of blotting out the color line in colleges, and has more Negro graduates by far than any other Northern college.

The total number of Negro college graduates up to 1899 (several of the graduates of that year not being reported) was as follows:

	Negro Colleges.	White Colleges.
Before '76	137	75
'75-80	143	22
'80-85	250	31
'85-90	413	43
'90-95	465	66
'95-99	475	88
Class Unknown	57	64
Total	1940	389

Of these graduates 2,079 were men and 252 were women; 50 per cent of northern-born college men come south to work among the masses of their people, at a sacrifice which few people realize; nearly 90 per cent of the southern-born graduates instead of seeking that personal freedom and broader intellectual atmosphere which their training has led them, in some degree, to conceive, stay and labor and wait in the midst of their black neighbors and relatives.

The most interesting question, and in many respects the crucial question, to be asked concerning college-bred Negroes, is: Do they earn a living? It has been intimated more than once that the higher training of Negroes has resulted in sending into the world of work men who could find nothing to do suitable to their talents. Now and then there comes a rumor of a colored college man working at menial service, etc. Fortunately, returns as to occupations of college-bred Negroes, gathered by the Atlanta conference, are quite full—nearly 60 per cent of the total number of graduates.

This enables us to reach fairly certain conclusions as to the occupations of all college-bred Negroes. Of 1,312 persons reported, there were:

	Per Cent
Teachers	53.4
Clergymen	16.8
Physicians, etc.	6.3
Students	5.6
Lawyers	4.7
In Govt. Service	4.0
In Business	3.6
Farmers and Artisans	2.7
Editors, Secretaries, and Clerks	2.4
Miscellaneous	.5

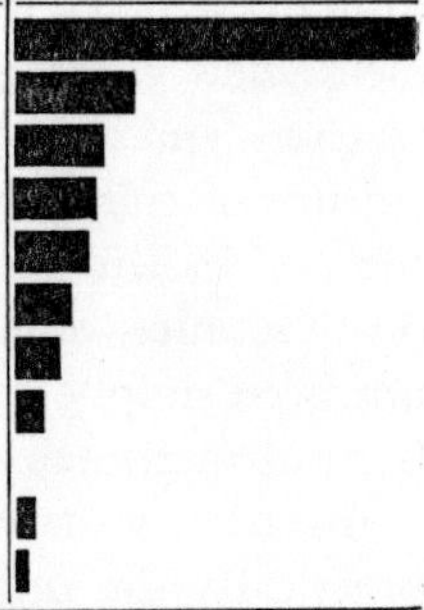

Over half are teachers, a sixth are preachers, another sixth are students and professional men; over 6 per cent are farmers, artisans, and merchants, and 4 per cent are in government service. . . .

These figures illustrate vividly the function of the college-bred Negro. He is, as he ought to be, the group leader, the man who sets the ideals of the community where he lives, directs its thoughts, and heads its social movements. It need hardly be argued that the Negro people need social leadership more than most groups; that they have no traditions to fall back upon, no long-established customs, no strong family ties, no well-defined social classes. All these things must be slowly and painfully evolved. The preacher was, even before the war, the group leader of the Negroes, and the church their greatest social institution. Naturally this preacher was ignorant and often immoral, and the problem of replacing the older type by better educated men has been a difficult one. Both by direct work and by direct influence on other preachers, and on congregations, the college-bred preacher has an opportunity for reformatory work and moral inspiration, the value of which cannot be overestimated.

It has, however, been in the furnishing of teachers that the Negro college has found its peculiar function. Few persons realize how vast a work, how mighty a revolution has been thus accomplished. To furnish five millions and more of ignorant people with teachers of their own race and blood, in one generation, was not only a very difficult undertaking, but a very important one, in that it placed before the eyes of almost every Negro child an attainable ideal. It brought the masses of the blacks in contact with modern civilization, made black men the leaders of their communities and trainers of the new generation. In this work college-bred Negroes were first teachers, and then teachers of teachers. And here it is that the broad culture of college work has been of peculiar value. Knowledge of life and its wider meaning has been the point of the Negro's deepest ignorance, and the sending out of teachers whose training has not been simply for breadwinning, but also for human culture, has been of inestimable value in the training of these men.

In earlier years the two occupations of preacher and teacher were practically the only ones open to the black college graduate. Of later years a larger diversity of life among his people has opened new avenues of employment. Nor have these college men been paupers and spendthrifts; 557 college-bred Negroes owned, in 1899, $1,342,862.50 worth of real estate (assessed value) or $2,411 per family. The real value of the total accumulations of the whole group is perhaps about $10,000,000, or $5,000 apiece. Pitiful, is it not, beside the fortunes of oil kings and steel trusts, but after all is the fortune of the millionaire the only stamp of true and successful living? Alas! it is, with many, and there's the rub.

The problem of training the Negro is today immensely complicated by the fact that the whole question of the efficiency and appropriateness of our present systems of education, for any kind of child, is a matter of active debate, in which final settlement seems still afar off. Consequently it often happens that persons arguing for or against certain systems of education for Negroes have these controversies in mind and miss the real question at issue. The main question, so far as the southern Negro is concerned, is: What, under the present circumstance, must a system of education do in order to raise the Negro as quickly as possible in the scale of civilization? The answer to this question seems to me clear: It must strengthen the Negro's character, increase his knowledge, and teach him to earn a living. Now it goes without saying, that it is hard to do all these things simultaneously or suddenly, and that at the same time it will not do to give all the attention to one and neglect the others; we could give black boys trades, but that alone will not civilize a race of ex-slaves; we might simply increase their knowledge of the world, but this would not necessarily make them wish to use this knowledge honestly; we might seek to strengthen character and purpose, but to what end if this people have nothing to eat or to wear? . . . Schoolhouses do not teach themselves—piles of brick and mortar and machinery do not send out *men*. It is the trained, living human soul, cultivated and strengthened by long study and thought, that breathes the real breath of life into boys and girls and makes them human, whether they be black or white, Greek, Russian, or American. Nothing, in these latter days, has so dampened the faith of thinking Negroes in recent educational movements as the fact that such movements have been accompanied by ridicule and denouncement and decrying of those very institutions of higher training which made the Negro public school possible, and make Negro industrial schools thinkable. It was Fisk, Atlanta, Howard, and Straight, those colleges born of the faith and sacrifice of the abolitionists, that placed in the black schools of the South the 30,000 teachers and more, which some, who depreciate the work of these higher schools, are using to teach their own new experiments. If Hampton, Tuskegee, and the hundred other industrial schools prove in the future to be as successful as they deserve to be, then their success in training black artisans for the South will be due primarily to the white colleges of the North and the black colleges of the South, which trained the teachers who today conduct these institutions. There was a time when the American people believed pretty devoutly that a log of wood with a boy at one end and Mark Hopkins at the other represented the highest ideal of human training. But in these eager days it would seem that we have changed all that and think it necessary to add a couple of saw mills and a hammer to this outfit, and, at a pinch, to dispense with the services of Mark Hopkins.

I would not deny, or for a moment seem to deny, the paramount necessity of teaching the Negro to work, and to work steadily and skillfully; or seem to depreciate in the slightest degree the important part industrial schools must play in the accomplishment of these ends, but I *do* say, and insist upon it, that it is industrialism drunk with its vision of success to imagine that its own work can be accomplished without providing for the training of broadly cultured men and women to teach its own teachers, and to teach the teachers of the public schools. . . .

I am an earnest advocate of manual training and trade teaching for black boys, and for white boys, too. I believe that next to the founding of Negro colleges the most valuable addition to Negro education since the war has been industrial training for black boys. Nevertheless, I insist that the object of all true education is not to make men carpenters, it is to make carpenters men; there are two means of making the carpenter a man, each equally important: the first is to give the group and community in which he works liberally trained teachers and leaders to teach him and his family what life means; the second is to give him sufficient intelligence and technical skill to make him an efficient workman; the first object demands the Negro college and college-bred men—not a quantity of such colleges, but a few of excellent quality; not too many college-bred men, but enough to leaven the lump, to inspire the masses, to raise the Talented Tenth to leadership; the second object demands a good system of common schools, well-taught, conveniently located, and properly equipped. . . .

What is the chief need for the building up of the Negro public school in the South? The Negro race in the South needs teachers today above all else. This is the concurrent testimony of all who know the situation. For the supply of this great demand two things are needed—institutions of higher education and money for schoolhouses and salaries. It is usually assumed that a hundred or more institutions for Negro training are today turning out so many teachers and college-bred men that the race is threatened with an oversupply. This is sheer nonsense. There are today less than 3,000 living Negro college graduates in the United States, and less than 1,000 Negroes in college. Moreover, in the 164 schools for Negroes, 95 per cent of their students are doing elementary and secondary work, work which should be done in the public schools. Over half the remaining 2,157 students are taking high-school studies. The mass of so-called "normal" schools for the Negro are simply doing elementary common-school work, or, at most, high-school work, with a little instruction in methods. The Negro colleges and the post-graduate courses at other institutions are the only agencies for the broader and more careful training of teachers. The work of these institutions is hampered for lack of funds. It is getting increasingly difficult to get funds for training teachers in the best modern methods, and yet all over the South, from state superintendents, county officials, city boards, and school principals comes the wail, "We need TEACHERS!" and teachers must be trained. As the fairest minded of all white southerners, Atticus G. Haygood, once said: "The defects of colored teachers are so great as to create an urgent necessity for training better ones. Their excellences and their successes are sufficient to justify the best hopes of success in the effort, and to vindicate the judgment of those who make large investments of money and service, to give to colored students opportunity for thoroughly preparing themselves for the work of teaching children of their people."

The truth of this has been strikingly shown in the marked improvement of white teachers in the South. Twenty years ago the rank and file of white public-school teachers were not as good as the Negro teachers. But they, by scholarships and good salaries, have been encouraged to thorough normal and collegiate preparation, while the Negro teachers have been discouraged by starvation wages and the idea that any training will do for a black teacher. . . .

Further than this, after being provided with group leaders of civilization, and a foundation of intelligence in the public schools, the carpenter, in order to be a man, needs technical skill. This calls for trade schools. Now trade schools are not nearly such simple things as people once thought. The original idea was that the "industrial" school was to furnish education, practically free, to those willing to work for it; it was to "do" things—i.e.: become a center of productive industry, it was to be partially, if not wholly, self-supporting, and it was to teach trades. Admirable as were some of the ideas underlying this scheme, the whole thing simply would not work in practice; it was found that if you were to use time and material to teach trades thoroughly, you could not at the same time keep the industries on a commercial basis and make them pay.

Many schools started out to do this on a large scale and went into virtual bankruptcy. Moreover, it was found also that it was possible to teach a boy a trade mechanically, without giving him the full educative benefit of the process, and, vice versa, that there was a distinctive educative value in teaching a boy to use his hands and eyes in carrying out certain physical processes, even though he did not actually learn a trade. It has happened, therefore, in the last decade, that a noticeable change has come over the industrial schools. In the first place the idea of commercially remunerative industry in a school is being pushed rapidly to the background. There are still schools with shops and farms that bring an income, and schools that use student labor partially for the erection of their buildings and the furnishing of equipment. It is coming to be seen, however, in the education of the Negro, as clearly as it has been seen in the education of the youths the world over, that it is the *boy,* and not the material product, that is the true object of education. Consequently the object of the industrial school came to be the thorough training of boys regardless of the cost of the training, so long as it was thoroughly well done.

Even at this point, however, the difficulties were not surmounted. In the first place modern industry has taken great strides since the war, and the teaching of trades is no longer a simple matter. Machinery and long processes of work have greatly changed the work of the carpenter, the ironworker, and the shoemaker. A really efficient workman must be today an intelligent man who has had good technical training in addition to thorough common-school, and perhaps even higher, training. To meet this situation the industrial schools began a further development; they established distinct trade schools for the thorough training of better class artisans, and at the same time they sought to preserve, for the purposes of general education, such of the simpler processes of elementary trade learning as were best suited therefor. In this differentiation of the trade school and manual training, the best of the industrial schools simply followed the plain trend of the present educational epoch. A prominent educator tells us that, in Sweden, "In the beginning the economic conception was generally adopted, and everywhere manual training was looked upon as a means of preparing the children of the common people to earn their living. But gradually it came to be recognized that manual training has a more elevated purpose, and one, indeed, more useful in the deeper meaning of the term. It came to be considered as an educative process for the complete moral, physical and intellectual development of the child."

Thus, again, in the manning of trade schools and manual-training schools we are thrown back upon the higher training as its source and chief support. There was a time when any aged and wornout carpenter could teach in a trade school. But not so today. Indeed the demand for college-bred men by a school like Tuskegee ought to make Mr. Booker T. Washington the firmest friend of higher training. Here he has as helpers the son of a Negro senator, trained in Greek and the humanities, and graduated at Harvard; the son of a Negro congressman and lawyer, trained in Latin and mathematics, and graduated at Oberlin; he has as his wife a woman who read Virgil and Homer in the same classroom with me; he has as college chaplain a classical graduate of Atlanta University; as teacher of science, a graduate of Fisk; as teacher of history, a graduate of Smith—indeed some thirty of his chief teachers are college graduates, and instead of studying French grammars in the midst of weeds, or buying pianos for dirty cabins, they are at Mr. Washington's right hand helping him in a noble work. And yet one of the effects of Mr. Washington's propaganda has been to throw doubt upon the expediency of such training for Negroes as these persons have had.

Men of America, the problem is plain before you. Here is a race transplanted through the criminal foolishness of your fathers. Whether you like it or not the millions are here, and here they will remain. If you do not lift them up, they will pull you down. Education and work are the levers to uplift a people. Work alone will not do it unless inspired by the right ideals and guided by intelligence. Education must not simply teach work—it must teach Life. The Talented Tenth of the Negro race must be made leaders of thought and missionaries of culture among their people. No others can do this work and Negro colleges must train men for it. The Negro race, like all other races, is going to be saved by its exceptional men.

Kelly Miller

For over fifty years, Dean Kelly Miller (1863?-1939), born in South Carolina, was identified with the growth and leadership of the outstanding Negro college, Howard University. Ascetic in habits and simple in tastes, he single-mindedly worked out the strategy of his race as well as its educational program. A great teacher, he decided to leave his chosen field of mathematics to help his people overcome their race problems. Presumably his lectures formed the basis of his two books, *Out of the House of Bondage* and *Race Adjustment,* as well as of innumerable articles about race relations. His forceful style, as the selection below shows, hit the mark in controversial literature.

Dean Miller was an expert consultant on Negro educational problems for the administrators of the public schools in the District of Columbia and for the General Education Board. The National Education Association sought him out as their chief speaker at a general session, and presidents, congressmen, and cabinet officials consulted him. The federal Commissioner of Education invited him to write a lengthy report in 1901 on almost all phases of Negro education; he wrote this report from a socially conscious viewpoint.

Compared with Du Bois, Miller was definitely a moderate, who saw much that was salvageable in the ideas of Booker T. Washington, who was a member of Howard's board of trustees and apparently a close friend of his. Washington, he felt, had to meet an entirely different situation than that confronting Douglass. Besides, he said, Washington "would not disclaim in distinct terms a single plank in the platform of Douglass."

This selection is from Kelly Miller's *Race Adjustment* (Neale, 1908), pp. 57-86. It is addressed to the demagogic John Temple Graves, editor of the *Atlanta News,* which ignited the bloody Atlanta Riot of September, 1906. Graves was a Bible literalist who urged that the race problem be solved by shipping all Negroes back to Africa.

An Appeal to Reason on the Race Problem: *An Open Letter to John Temple Graves Suggested by the Atlanta Riot*

October, 1906

Mr. John Temple Graves,
Atlanta, Georgia

My Dear Sir: The world has read with horror of the Atlanta massacre and of the part you played during that awful hour. The outbreak is but the fruits of the seeds of race wrath which you and others have been assiduously sowing. They who sow the wind may expect to reap the whirlwind.

Your open appeal to the passion of the American people while this riot was yet at its height was fraught with evil suggestiveness. That half the people of Atlanta were not slain is due to the fact that other counsel than yours prevailed. The rabble is ever actuated by sinister influence. It obeys the acquiescent nod of secret understanding. There is a wireless communication between the baser elements of society and the cunning instigator who provokes them to wrath. Shakespeare with inimitable faithfulness has described the inner workings of this subtle and guilty control whereby the obsequious is prone to take the humor of the mighty for a warrant "to break within the bloody house of life" on the winking of authority.

After a wide scanning of the American press, yours is the only voice which I have heard, south or north, white or black, still breathing out hatred and slaughter amidst this awful carnival of blood. You alone occupy that "bad eminence." You broke the unanimity of appeal to reason when wild passion had reached its whitest heat.

Your attitude contrasted with that of the foremost member of the afflicted race measures the whole diameter of difference between cruelty and mercy. While Negroes, innocent of any crime, were suffering torture which would cause even the bruised worm to turn, Booker T. Washington, with Christ-like forgiveness of spirit, counseled his people to resist not evil.

The natural impulse of one belonging to the victim race is to indulge in indignant and bitter words. It is almost impossible to repress this natural ebullition of feeling. When human nature is so flagrantly outraged the very stones would cry out if men should hold their peace. It requires the highest self-repression and poise of spirit to refrain from verbal vehemence. But the voice of wisdom counsels only such expression as will tend to relieve rather than to intensify the strain of a critical situation.

I wish to utilize this gruesome occasion to discuss in an epistolary form some of the issues growing out of race relations in this country. I shall strive to be entirely courteous and considerate, and yet I shall abate no whit the fullest candor and plainness of statement demanded of one who speaks for the best interest of his people. Even an ambassador in bonds should speak with becoming boldness. There is a lamentable lack of expression which is at once candid and considerate, as respects the attitude of one race toward the other. We are prone to indulge in either wild, ungoverned onslaught, or diplomatic dissimulation and prudential concealment of real opinion and feeling. Honesty of utterance is usually accompanied with such ruthless and brutal frankness on the one hand, and resentful defiance on the other, as to render rational discussion impossible; while considerate temperament is too often given to indulgence in such fulsome flattery or unmanly yieldance as to make wholesome discussion unprofitable. Several years ago I sat on the platform of a meeting in Atlanta composed of about equal numbers of the two races. If I mistake not, you were present on that occasion. Local representatives on both sides of the race line vied with each other in vowing racial affection and ties of endearment. Words could go no further in expressing friendly relationship. But as I sat there, I divined, as I thought, a hidden spirit not revealed in the spoken words, which seemed to me to be simply verbal civilities and diplomatic platitudes. When the meeting adjourned each went to his own company with no surer knowledge of the real feeling or purpose of the other than when it convened.

Mr. Thomas Nelson Page has suggested in his recent book that the time has come for the best representatives of both races to meet together in conference on matters vitally concerning the common weal. It is needless to say that the value of such conference will depend upon the candor and frankness of spirit on both sides. The strained relation between the races calls for the temper and spirit of a statesmanship which discards wild hysterics and the heated passion of the moment, and sanely safeguards the interests of all the people. We are confronted with a problem whose factors are as intricate and whose outcome is as far-reaching as any that has ever taxed human wisdom for solution.

I am addressing this letter to you not merely because of the leading part which you played in the recent eruption, but also because you stand for a policy and a propaganda whose fatuity it fully reveals. It is a dangerous thing to arouse the evil spirit. It will turn again and rend you. The recent Atlanta outbreak fully illustrates the folly of appealing to the baser passion, especially in a particolored community.

Have you stopped to consider the cause and outcome of Atlanta's shame? The State of Georgia had been lashed into fury for more than a year of bitter race discussion. The atmosphere was ominous and tense. The fuse was ready for the spark. There were assaults or rumors of assaults by black or blackened fiends, upon white women, in and around Atlanta. These were eagerly seized upon and exaggerated by an inflammatory press. They became the alarum and rallying cry about which the pent-up wrath of race found vent. Red journalism ran rife. The terrorized imaginations saw a fiend incarnate in every darksome face. One paper, a little redder than the rest, boldly offered a reward for a lynching bee in the capital of the Empire State of the South. The flaring headlines fanned the fire into a furious flame. The evil passion of a people always finds lodgment in the breasts of its basest members. The half-grown, half-drunk, half-savage descendants of Oglethorpe's colonists can no longer contain themselves. Like the Indian on the war-path, they must have a savage yell. "Kill the Negro brutes!" is the tocsin. They kill and beat and bruise Negroes on sight. The air is filled with ghoulish yells, mingled with the shrieks and groans of the mangled and dying. Although the hollow cry of virtue is ever on the lip, the mob has no more conception of righteousness than a bloodhound set upon a scent cares about the guilt or innocence of his quarry. The aroused appetite for blood must be satiated. The police sprinkle the mob with the water hose; but they laugh at this complaisant impotency and joke with the mayor over the awful deeds of death, and cry out louder for blood. The Negroes are in seclusion; the liquor dens are closed; red headlines are suppressed in the local press. The fury of the mob ceases when it has nothing further to feed on. Twenty innocent Negroes are dead. The guilty escape amid the slaughter of the innocent. Not a single criminal has been touched. No evil propensity has been eradicated. As the spasm of delirium relaxes the city's name stands tarnished before the world. The sin of it, the shame of it will abide for many a day. The Negroes emerge bleeding and torn; the whites are dumbfounded at the evil possibilities of their baser class. The race problem still remains unsolved and the remedy for evil unsuggested. No knot is untied in the tangled web. Such is the fatuity of your doctrine that the Negro must be controlled through the terror of the senses.

Atlanta may be regarded as the Athens of the South. It abounds in schools and colleges for both races. Here is the home of many of the most illustrious names in the South. Here lived the late Henry W. Grady, the oracle of the New South. Joel Chandler Harris and Clark Howell wield a journalistic and literary influence second to none of that section. Among the Negroes Atlanta is noted for its increasing class of cultivated and refined people. Bowen, Du Bois, and Crogman are men of light and leading, whose influence and power for good have gone out to all the land; and yet deliberate appeal to race passion may involve this community, with so many influences of refinement and restraint, in riot and ruin in a single night.

While the Atlanta riot still raged, a hurricane was blowing up from the tropics which destroyed hundreds of lives and millions of property in several southern cities. But there was no blood-guiltiness. These cities will bury their dead and rebuild their waste places and pursue their path of peace and progress, forgetful and unregretful of this disastrous touch of nature. But the stain of Atlanta will abide. Immigration and capital will shun a mob-ruled city as they would a place infected with pestilence and death. The evil passion of man is more to be dreaded than the terror of earthquake or storm.

You represent the ultra type of opinion and feeling which find lodgment in the breast of the lower order of your own race. You would shut the Negro out from competition on the narrow and intolerant theory that there may not be enough "for you and us." Fearful that the tree of civilization is not big enough to bear fruit for all, you would deny the black man the God-given right to stretch forth his hand and partake of its fullness.

You are a disciple of Senator Tillman, who is the guide, philosopher, and friend of those who worship at the shrine of racial narrowness and hate.

Mr. William Garrott Brown, a scion of the traditional South, tells us in his most interesting book on "The Lower South in American History" that "the triumph of the Tillmanites in South Carolina worked a change in the internal policies of that State deeper than the change in 1776 and 1860." When we study the deep significance of the Tillman movement, we find that these words convey only the sober truth. The Tillman influence is by no means limited to his own state, but is equally potent in all parts of the South. . . .

I beg to suggest that in dealing with the southern situation you look upon the task as a race problem, rather than as a human problem. The human aspect is ignored and the racial feature overemphasized. We have before us a dual problem of the perfectibility of the people, and of racial peace and harmony.

The South is freighted with an awful load of ignorance and poverty, and resultant degradation. Much of this attaches to the white race, but more to the Negro. There are no nostrums or miracles that will roll away this reproach. It requires the united effort of all the nation to enlighten, upbuild, and adjust these neglected people. A wise and far-seeing statesmanship would not seek to isolate and perpetuate these incapacities in one race, but would banish them entirely. Unless ignorance and poverty are destroyed, they will rise up ever and anon to perplex and to trouble. Ignorance and vice are not racial attributes; knowledge and virtue are not racial endowments; they are the outcome of condition. Crime has no color; the criminal no race; he is the common enemy of society. He should be isolated and dealt with according to the desert of his evil deed. It is folly to punish a race for the wrongdoings of an individual. The enlightened elements of both races should make common cause with knowledge against ignorance, with virtue against vice, and with law against the lawless.

I must not close this letter without expressing the firm conviction that Negroes of light and leading have grave and serious responsibility. Their race is the victim in every conflict. While they cannot restrain the hardened criminal without governmental authority, yet they are in duty bound to put forth strenuous efforts to reach and to influence for good the weak, helpless, and neglected elements of their own race, and to keep them from falling into evil ways. There is a subtle sympathy of race which renders individuals more easily amenable to the moral control of those of their own blood. The Negro schoolteacher and minister of the gospel stand in the high place of moral authority. They should utilize all the power which they are permitted to wield, and by example, precept, and persuasion sustain their weaker brethren in all right directions. They must bridge over the widening chasm between the educated and the more unfortunate by a practical sympathy and a more vital and brotherly touch. In this great work of human development we ask and should receive the hearty good will and cooperation of all those who believe in the perfectibility of man. The Negro is impressionable and responsive to kind treatment. If given the necessary encouragement he will become a safe, conservative factor, and not the economic or moral menace which you so vociferously proclaim him to be. It will not be necessary to ruthlessly override all human and divine order at the behest of the narrow racial arrogance. All far-seeing and conservative Americans believe that in the final outcome peace and good will, friendship and amity will prevail, and that "Ephraim shall not envy Judah, and Judah shall not vex Ephraim. . . ."

James Weldon Johnson

In the militant literary tradition of Douglass and Du Bois was James Weldon Johnson (1871-1938), who came up from the South in 1901 to the fast-growing Negro city of Harlem. He was born in Jacksonville, Florida, the son of the headwaiter of the city's chief hotel and a cultured mother attached to music, drawing, and books. Always a very bright student, he finished his education at Atlanta University and then taught in a backward little Negro school in Georgia. After serving as principal of a Jacksonville elementary and high school, he took up the law as a profession, but then gave it up to join his musically gifted brother for a career in New York City's theatrical world.

In Harlem he met the kindly Paul Lawrence Dunbar, whose racially conscious poems and short stories in dialect had fascinated William Dean Howells and countless readers of both races. Soon Johnson was following in Dunbar's steps and in his writing went even beyond him in penetrating the folk life, idiom, and ideals of the Negro people—without depending upon misspelling for effect, although he may have lacked the older man's sophisticated rhythms. After all, he had more intimate contact with the southern Negro than did Dunbar of Ohio. In *God's Trombones* he pictured a gentle Negro God who decided upon Creation with the words, "I'm lonely—I'll make me a world." Johnson loved to interpret the informal Negro preacher and the spontaneous charm of his people, especially in their spirituals, which he collected.

In those years in Harlem he wrote many lyrical hits to his brother's music and had the satisfaction of seeing the poem he had written for his Jacksonville schoolchildren, "Lift Every Voice and Sing," eventually become known as the Negro's national hymn. He studied drama at Columbia University and wrote successful musical comedies and the English libretto for *Goyescas,* which was performed at the Metropolitan Opera. He was also active in politics, campaigning for the re-election of Roosevelt and these efforts undoubtedly led to his appointment as consul in Venezuela and Nicaragua. He found time also to write his revealing novel, *The Autobiography of an Ex-Colored Man* (1912), a pioneer treatment of the fascinating phenomenon of Negro "passing." For a time he edited one of the oldest Negro newspapers, *The New York Age*.

By 1916 Johnson had turned his efforts to race relations. As a very active field secretary of the NAACP, he greatly increased the membership of that young organization, bravely investigated lynchings first-hand in southern towns—as the selection below shows—organized protest demonstrations in various celebrated causes, and fought major cases for civil liberties. In 1920 he investigated abuses in Haiti under American occupation on behalf of the NAACP; he charged that the Marines had killed 3,000 Haitians, thus helping to create a major issue in a presidential election. He became an attractive symbol of the New Negro—an independent man free from traditional servility—in the Negro Renaissance of the Twenties, and he won the coveted Spingarn Medal for his work in combatting anti-Negro persecution.

This selection, dealing with Johnson's field experiences in the South, reveals his sensitive understanding of race relations, particularly of the tacit conspiracy to conceal the facts of lynching, and his artistic appreciation of the old Negro preacher and the trusting response of the southern Negro. It is drawn from his highly readable autobiography, *Along This Way* (New York: The Viking Press, Inc., 1933), pp. 329-335. Copyright 1933 by James Weldon Johnson; © 1961 by Grace Nail Johnson. Reprinted here by permission of The Viking Press, Inc.

Along This Way

With the opening of 1918, Mr. White, as assistant secretary, and Mr. Shillady, as the new secretary, came to the Association; and my individual responsibility and work were lessened. Mr. Shillady had great ability as a systematizer and organizer. He laid out the work of the increasing staff according to the most modern and approved methods. He planned a national drive for membership that was eminently successful. And he conducted the first adequate statistical study of lynching ever made. He sent two research workers to the Congressional Library at Washington, who read the newspapers back over a period of thirty years and extracted the data regarding every lynching that had been published. They set down the names, sex, and age of the victim; the place, date, and manner of each lynching; and the charge upon which each victim was lynched. These data were compiled and tabulated by Mr. Shillady, and published in a book of over a hundred pages, under the title of *Thirty Years of Lynching in the United States.* The most startling fact revealed was that the common opinion that Negroes were lynched only for rape was without foundation. The figures showed that of the more than three thousand Negroes lynched in the thirty-year period, less than 17 per cent had even been charged with rape. They showed that Negroes had been lynched for "talking back" to white persons, for "not driving out of the road" to let white persons pass. They also showed that more than fifty Negro women had been lynched, against whom, of course, the "usual crime" could not be charged. This publication was of a value beyond estimation in the Association's fight against lynching. The Association began to take on magnitude. The office staff was added to. H. J. Seligmann was taken on as Director of Publicity, and William Pickens, already widely known as an orator, was taken on as Associate Field Secretary. The clerical staff in the office was increased to a dozen or more persons.

Very early in the year I went on the road speaking and organizing. The field was ready to be harvested. The war and the exodus had shaken the Negroes of the entire country loose from their traditional moorings of standpatism and timidity. They were awake and eager. My speaking was not confined to the colored people; in the North, I addressed many white audiences.

The experiences that came to me through these meetings were varied; some of them thrilling, some pathetic, and some humorous. I remember how the pathos of one situation gripped me. I was addressing a white forum in a midwestern industrial city, which, at that time, had only a very small Negro population. As is generally the case under such conditions, these people were disoriented. But a delegation of them waited on me when I had finished my address, and asked if I would not come and speak to a meeting of colored people and organize them into a branch of the Association. It was late, but, when I learned that an audience was waiting for me in the little colored church, I went. When I reached the church, I found it jammed to suffocation. As I went up the aisle to the pulpit, there was no applause—a demonstration I had become accustomed to—the people seemed to regard me with a worshipful silence, as though I were some sort of messiah. When I spoke to them, they hung on my words with such confidence and childlike faith that I could have wept, wept because of my own lack of power to deliver them.

In my trip through the Middle West, I reached a large colored church one Sunday morning and found that the whole service had been turned over to me. I was sitting with the pastor in his study waiting for the time to begin, when he asked me what my text was to be. I stammered that I really had no text, and that I was going to make a talk, not deliver a sermon. "But," he demanded, "aren't you a preacher?" I had to admit that I was not. He grew angry at my admission, and spoke to me as though he had been taken in. He declared that he could not allow any secular topic to take the place of the regular morning service. I told him there were phases of my subject that had a decidedly spiritual bearing, and that I did not think his congregation would consider them out of place. He reluctantly yielded, and did so, I felt, really because he had counted on a Sunday morning off and had not prepared a sermon.

The error this pastor had made in considering me a clergyman was based on a double confusion. I was frequently referred to in the newspapers, and introduced to audiences (incorrectly) as "ex-Minister to Venezuela and Nicaragua," and to many people, "preacher" comes up spontaneously as the synonym for "minister." In fact, after my engagement to Grace became known, one of her admirers called her up to josh her about the absurd rumor he had heard that she was going to marry a preacher.

I found that the matter of professional titles was not a minor one in many a place where I spoke. At a meeting in a southern city, the preacher who was down on the program to make the remarks that would introduce me to the audience leaned over, as we sat on the platform, and whispered. "What might be your entitlements?" "No entitlements," I whispered back, "just Mister. Introduce me as Mr. Johnson." With deep sincerity he whispered back again, "I can't do it. I can't introduce you to these people as just Mister." And he didn't; he introduced me as "Professor Johnson."

My meetings quite commonly served a double purpose; an occasion for me to make a speech on the work of the Association and to organize a branch or add to membership; and an opportunity for local talent, especially musical talent, to display itself. Good music helped a meeting, if it was not too good, and if there was not too much of it. For the main purpose of the meeting I preferred spirited singing by the audience to solos by individual artists. One soloist, however, I shall never forget. He was a powerful, ebony-hued baritone who unwittingly metamorphosed *Danny Deever* into a stirring race song by dramatically declaiming:

> 'What makes that rear-rank breathe so 'ard?'
> Said Files-on-Parade.
> 'It's bitter cold, it's bitter cold,'
> The *colored* sergeant said.

I received once a laboriously written and marvelously spelled letter. The writer assured me that he had heard a great deal about me and the wonderful society for the advancement of colored people of which I was "the head." He informed me that he was colored and that the state of his affairs had reached a point so low as to be critical; and concluded with the request that I *advance him* about ten dollars.

My work on the road carried me into the far South, and I had opportunity to observe closely the operation of two powerful forces that were at work on the Negro's status—the exodus and the war. Negroes were migrating to the North in great numbers, and I observed the anomaly of a premium being put on this element of the population that had generally been regarded as a burden and a handicap to the South. Here, it seemed, was a splendid chance to get rid of a lot of "lazy, worthless people," but some communities were so loath to lose them that they obliged railroad ticket agents to adopt a policy of not selling tickets to Negroes to go North. In many instances Negroes were forcibly restrained from leaving.

The demands of the war were also working great changes. A train that I was on stopped at Waycross, Georgia. I saw a great crowd around the station and on the tracks, and got out of my coach to see what it was all about. I found a long train loaded with Negro troops who were on their way "over there," and witnessed the incredible sight of white women, together with colored women, all dressed alike in a Red Cross looking uniform, busy distributing to the men neatly wrapped packages of whatever things such committees gave to soldiers leaving for the front.

I reached Jacksonville a day or two before the date of a mass meeting that was being held in the National Guard armory. Let me here go back to a time when I was in Jacksonville three or four years prior to this meeting. The armory, built, of course, out of the tax funds of Duval County, was then brand-new. The drill room was the finest and largest auditorium in Jacksonville; its use as a municipal auditorium was among the advantages set forth in the project for building the armory. Its first use under this head was for a musical affair that had been promoted by a committee of white women. These ladies had arranged to have Coleridge-Taylor's *Hiawatha* sung, and for the principal role had engaged a tenor from Atlanta. A small group of colored people wanted very much to hear the cantata, and they asked me if I would not see if it could be arranged for them to do so. I telephoned Mrs. Lund, who was on the committee, and stated the case. She seemed very much pleased that there were colored people who wanted to hear the class of music that was to be sung. She asked how many there would be. I told her, probably twenty-five. She assured me that seats would be arranged for them and they would be welcome. The group was delighted. They asked me if I was going with them. I answered that I had been lucky enough to hear *Hiawatha* under better circumstances, and would not go. The next day, Mrs. Lund rang me up. She was very much perturbed. She gave me to know that the militia officer in charge of the armory had countermanded the arrangements that had been made; he had declared that Negroes could not be allowed in the armory. I asked Mrs. Lund if she thought the militia officer knew that the music to be sung was the work of a Negro composer. She did not answer that. Indeed, it is doubtful whether Mrs. Lund, as competent a musician as she was, or any other lady of the committee, knew that Coleridge-Taylor was a Negro.

The mass meeting that was to be held at the armory was for the purpose of stimulating the sale of Liberty Bonds. Fully a half of the auditorium was filled with colored people, and they subscribed liberally. On the platform was a large committee composed of white and colored citizens. Both white and colored speakers addressed the audience. By the white speakers, especially, great emphasis was laid on "*our* country" and "what *we* must do" to win the war for democracy. I don't know whether the same militia officer was still in charge of the armory or not.

But all of the forces were not favorable. These changes that I have alluded to were, after all, slight in proportion to the underlying mass of prejudice and bigotry. The Ku Klux Klan was beginning to gain the tremendous power it possessed a year or so later; and clouds were gathering that, within twelve months, would blot the light from the skies for the Negro. It was while I was in Jacksonville on this trip that I received a letter from Mr. Shillady asking me to go to Quitman, Georgia, and talk with a young colored man who knew a great deal about the "Mary Turner lynching," and to try and have him come on to New York. Walter White had, a short while before, investigated this lynching and reported that this young colored man had driven the wagon of the white undertaker who took charge of the bodies of the victims; and that he, probably, could divulge the names of some of the members of the mob. Mr. White's investigation of this lynching, one of the most monstrous in all the records, made a national sensation. It was his first important job in this work for which he was so well fitted; not the least of his advantages being that his race could not be detected from his appearance.

I proceeded to Quitman, arriving late in the afternoon. I went to the house of a colored doctor. He was fearful; so much so that he communicated his fears to me. He said that the town was still alive over the lynching, and much incensed over Mr. White's disclosures; and that it would not be safe for me to go out that night, because my appearance in a town the size of Quitman would be sure to arouse suspicion. He put out all the lights in the house at about nine o'clock and we went to bed. I did not sleep. The slightest sound gave me a start, for I could not but judge that the doctor's precautions were necessary. The very fact that he had taken me in was proof that he was no coward.

The next day I started out to find my young man. I found him in one of those dingy restaurants for Negroes, common in the South. He told me that his mother ran the place. It was located in the Negro quarter. There were ill-kept tables in the front, and a battered pool table in the back. I talked with him a long while, using all the persuasion I could bring to bear to have him consent to come North and state all he knew about the lynching, or give me the names of such members of the mob as he knew. He refused to do either. He said that if he went North, he would leave his mother at the mercies of the lynchers; and if he gave me the names, suspicion would point directly to him. The common sense of the position he took was unassailable.

While I was talking with him, an automobile drove up at the front. It was a small roadster or coupé, but it was loaded down with six men, all white. They were a pretty tough-looking lot. They called for the young fellow to come out. He said to me, "There they are now. What'll I tell 'em if they ask about you?" I did not see how they could know that I was in town, but I told him to say what I had told the doctor to say, in case of any questions—that I was taking subscriptions for a colored newspaper. He went out, and remained talking with the men longer than was pleasant for me. When he came in, he summed up what the men had said to him into—"They asked me what you were doing here, and I told them you were taking subscriptions. They told me to keep my damned mouth shut."

I got out of Quitman that afternoon and I did not feel safe or comfortable until the train had crossed the Florida line.

At a meeting that I addressed in one of the Western cities, I received the impulse to make a definite start on a piece of literary work I had long been nursing in my mind. I had long been planning that at some time I should take the primitive stuff of the old-time Negro sermon and, through art-governed expression, make it into poetry. I felt that this primitive stuff could be used in a way similar to that in which a composer makes use of a folk theme in writing a major composition. I believed that the characteristic qualities: imagery, color, abandon, sonorous diction, syncopated rhythms, and native idioms, could be preserved and, at the same time, the composition as a whole be enlarged beyond the circumference of mere race, and given universality. These ideas I had revolved, but I had not yet set myself to the task of working them out. For several years, I had been excusing myself on the ground of not having time.

It was Sunday, and I had been addressing meetings in various colored churches. I had finished my fourth talk, and it was after nine o'clock at night. However, to my surprise and irritation, the local committee informed me that I was scheduled for still another address. I protested the lateness of the hour, but was told that for the meeting at this church we were just in good time.

When we reached the church an "exhorter" was concluding a dull sermon. I was ushered to the platform, where I sat and listened to two more short, uninteresting efforts. These were but preliminaries, curtain-raisers, for the main event, a sermon by a famed evangelist.

At last he rose. He was a dark brown man, handsome in his gigantic proportions. I think the presence of a "distinguished visitor" on the platform disconcerted him a bit, for he started in to preach a formal sermon from a formal text. He was flat. The congregation sat apathetic and dozing. He must have realized that he was neither impressing the "distinguished visitor" nor giving the congregation what it expected; for, suddenly and without any warning for the transition, he slammed the Bible shut, stepped out from behind the pulpit, and began intoning the rambling Negro sermon that begins with the creation of the world, touches various high spots in the trials and tribulations of the Hebrew children, and ends with the Judgment Day. There was an instantaneous change in the preacher and in the congregation. He was free, at ease, and the complete master of himself and his hearers. The congregation responded to him as a willow to the winds. He strode the pulpit up and down, and brought into play the full gamut of a voice that excited my envy. He intoned, he moaned, he pleaded—he blared, he crashed, he thundered. A woman sprang to her feet, uttered a piercing scream, threw her handbag to the pulpit, striking the preacher full in the chest, whirled round several times, and fainted. The congregation reached a state of ecstasy. I was fascinated by this exhibition; moreover, something primordial in me was stirred. Before the preacher finished, I took a slip of paper from my pocket and somewhat surreptitiously jotted down some ideas for my first poem.

It had been thirty years since I had heard such a sermon. I still had my somewhat vague, youthful memories; but this fresh exhibition of the potentialities of the material I planned to use was just what I needed to start me on the work. In the course of several weeks, I finished "The Creation" to my satisfaction. It was published in *The Freeman*.

In writing "The Creation," I had to consider a question that had to be settled then and there for the whole group of poems—the question of form and medium. I at once discarded the use of conventionalized Negro dialect, for reasons which I set forth fully in the Preface to the poems when they were published in book form.[1] Furthermore, it was not my intention to paint the picturesque or comic aspects of the old-time Negro preacher—I considered them extraneous—my aim was to interpret what was in his mind, to express, if possible, the dream to which, despite limitations, he strove to give utterance. I chose a loose rhythmic instead of a strict metric form, because it was the first only that could accommodate itself to the movement, the abandon, the changes of tempo, and the characteristic syncopations of the primitive material.

In "The Creation" I was happy over the results of my experiments. Following its publication in *The Freeman,* it received numerous commendations. It has since been included in a dozen or more anthologies. One of the first to pronounce the poem an excellent one was William Stanley Braithwaite, with whom in these years I had formed a close and helpful friendship. I was happy, too, over the fact that I had at last made an opening on this piece of work. . . .

[1] *God's Trombones—Seven Negro Sermons in Verse.* New York, The Viking Press, 1927.

Carter G. Woodson

While few Negro intellectuals could boast of a mass following, Dr. Carter G. Woodson (1875-1950) of Washington, D.C., influenced many thousands of teachers and schoolchildren to study Negro history and to appreciate their ties to an African past. He was born in New Canton, Virginia, on December 19, 1875, but moved to Huntington, West Virginia, in 1892 where he labored in the coal mines and picked up his early education at night. After a few sessions at the interracial Berea College, he was able to get a B.A. (1907) and an M.A. (1908) at the University of Chicago. Meanwhile, he supported himself as a high-school principal, a schoolteacher, a dean of Howard University's School of Liberal Arts, a dean of West Virginia Collegiate Institute, and, most important, as editor of the *Journal of Negro History,* published in Washington, D.C. His emphatic views often brought him into collision with superiors and colleagues, although he was essentially a kindly, thoughtful person.

His doctoral dissertation at Harvard, *The Disruption of Virginia,* prepared him for his decision to devote a lifetime to historical research conceived as a means for the liberation of his people. On October 9, 1915 he organized the Association for the Study of Negro Life and History with the objective of collecting "sociological and historical data on the Negro, the study of peoples of African blood, the publishing of books in this field and the promotion of harmony between the races by acquainting one with the achievements of the other." The following January he established the scholarly *Journal of Negro History* with an editorial board drawn from both races. His goal was to demonstrate that Negroes had always played a substantial part in shaping their own destiny.

A prolific writer, he published some thirty books, especially textbooks for Negro history courses. His original researches established some significant generalizations, notably regarding the small class of free Negro owners of slaves, the importance of the African past, Negro migrations, the role of Negro churches, and other facets of Negro life. He made Negro History Week important not only for schoolchildren but for scholars as well, and this annual institution provided a forum, especially on the eve of the

Negro Revolution of the 1960's, for a discussion of historical Negro tactics in the search for equality. Sound history did not seem to him incompatible with useful propaganda for social action.

The following selection, "History Made to Order," is taken from the *Journal of Negro History*, Vol. 12 (1927), 330-341, and is reproduced with the generous permission of the publication's editors. It clearly reflects Dr. Woodson's interpretations as well as his crusading temperament. Noteworthy in this article are his explanation of the anomaly of Negro slaveholding, his refutation of the current tendency to minimize slave exploitation, and his evaluation of the strategy of the abolitionist movement.

History Made to Order

The following letter, addressed to a reader of apparently good intentions, points out the danger resulting from the bias which permeates the so-called histories of our time:

March 5, 1927

Mr. G. D. Eaton
204 West 13th St.
New York City

My dear Mr. Eaton:

I have read your article on slavery and abolition entitled "Horrors Made to Order," which appeared in the February issue of *McNaught's Monthly*. Inasmuch as I am quoted in support of your unwarranted deduction and distortion of facts, I consider it my duty to address you this open letter.

The most flagrant errors which you made in your paper are an exaggeration of the number of slaves who had to return from persecution in the North to yield to slavery in the South, too much emphasis on the isolated cases of the interest of southerners in emancipation, a minimization of the horrors of slavery, a misrepresentation of the church as it developed in the slaveholding South, and an unwarranted attack on the abolitionists. Considered in detail, however, your errors are too numerous to be mentioned in a letter; and, since some of your statements refute themselves, they require no answer from the undersigned.

You are unfortunate in failing to understand that slavery differed from period to period in this country, and differed further in its aspects from country to country during the same period. In fact, the first Negroes brought to this country were not slaves. They were indentured servants and became gradually debased to the lower status. At that time, slavery was unknown to English law. Slavery in the West Indies was not the same as slavery in the colonies along the Atlantic Coast, and slavery in its beginnings in America differed widely from what it was when it was finally abolished. Slavery differed from plantation to plantation, too, because each slaveholder was a law unto himself and could make it anything he wanted. Like the six men who visited the elephant, then, one can make almost any sort of argument with respect to slavery.

At this point uninformed writers do the cause of truth unusual harm. Finding a few treatises on slavery during the earliest period, they refer to the institution as strictly patriarchal and wonder why abolitionists were so unwise as to attack it. On the other hand, other unfortunates may discover treatises dealing with the institution during its most cruel development and may radically denounce it in terms more scathing than it is portrayed in abolition literature. An historical student, however, understands how to consider an institution according to its cycles of development and the standard of its time.

The question as to whether or not slavery in the United States was cruel, moreover, results merely from the difference in points of view. Pagan historians of our time insist that slavery was a benevolent institution. The god of race superiority ordained that the one race should be subjugated to serve the other. The Negro, therefore, was at fault in resisting his enslavement. His master in whipping him or even killing him if he resisted was doing no wrong, for slavery could not have been maintained any other way, and it had to be maintained. Classifying Negroes as animals, too, such authors find that the masters were often indulgent and kind to the slaves. The slaves cost more to support and caused so much more trouble than horses and mules. Yet the slaves were given more consideration. Whereas the resistance of the horses and mules never got beyond that of a little kicking back, the slaves sometimes fought their masters or started insurrections among their fellows. These writers naturally think that the masters did unusually well under the circumstances.

Enlightened people, however, do not understand how there can be any justice in enslaving one race to another to establish its monopoly of all the good things of this world. Civilized people can see no justice in beating or killing a man because he will not do the will of another. Man should not exercise power over another except for altruistic purposes. There was no wisdom in keeping the Negro in drudgery and darkness under the false notion of keeping the white man in a higher realm, for ultimately the system meant ruin to the white man as well. To maintain the institution there must be someone brutal enough to beat and kill an unoffending people. To have slavery there must be an enslaver. To have murder there must be a murderer. The reform element insisted that we should not have either.

Your misuse of facts becomes decidedly astounding when one reads that 40,000 free Negroes owned nearly 100,000 slaves. I doubt that a more mischievous exaggeration has ever been written. Some years ago, the Association for the Study of Negro Life and History made a careful study of the Negro ownership of slaves in the United States, recorded in the Census Reports of 1830, and found that 3,777 free Negroes actually owned 12,920 slaves, an average of less than four to each Negro slaveholder. Unless these numbers increased by leaps and bounds during the next three decades, they could not have reached the estimate you have made. As a matter of fact, the number of Negro slaveholders tended to decrease proportionately after 1830. Laws made it more difficult for Negroes to acquire slave property because it brought such Negroes too near to the status of white men.

Most of these cases of Negro slaveholding, moreover, were not primarily for the purpose of exploitation. There were a few southern Negroes who had considerable land. To develop this land they had to use laborers and the easiest way to supply the demand was through the purchase of slaves. The large majority of the Negroes who owned slaves, however, were engaged in it from a benevolent point of view. Free Negroes often purchased slaves to make their lot easier by granting them their freedom for a nominal sum or by permitting them to work it out on liberal terms. In many cases, a husband purchased the wife or vice versa. The children of such unions, therefore, became slaves. After the reactionary measures in the South made it unlawful for a free Negro to remain in certain States unless he could give bond or by special act of the state legislature had been permitted to remain, it was deemed unwise for Negro slaveholding husbands or wives to manumit their own relatives. If they had done so, these slaves on becoming free would have been compelled to leave the state. They could not easily establish themselves in strange communities. In treating this exceptional history of the Negro, therefore, you have made the blunder of emphasizing the exception rather than the rule.

It is true that at the time of the immigration of the Germans and Scotch-Irish into this country during the Thirties, Forties, and Fifties, it was difficult for the free Negroes migrating from the South to the North to find employment. Most of these foreigners were common laborers. Competing with these elements in menial service, the Negro migrants became an object of attacks by mobs and some few of them found it so unpleasant that they had to return to the land of slavery. However, it is a misrepresentation to refer to these unfortunates as an unusual number. The actual figures published by the Census Bureau showing the large number of free Negroes who, in spite of this condition, moved to the North and settled there is ample refutation of your statement. They could easily find labor in the South inasmuch as the southern whites were trying to make their living from the labor of others rather than indulge in drudgery themselves. After all, moreover, our history shows that the economic factor is the most important one in determining whether persecuted people will bear the ills they have rather than fly to those they know not of.

You are wrong in your estimate of the southern sentiment in behalf of abolition after the rise of the cotton kingdom. You do not seem to know that such abolition sentiment as is usually accredited to the South was restricted largely to the Appalachian Highland, which extended like a northern peninsula into a proslavery South.

This section of the South was settled by Scotch-Irish Presbyterians and Germans, who, in coming to the South after the slaveholders had preempted the fertile lands in the tidewater district, had to settle in the uplands and in the mountains of the seaboard states. Having come from Europe, where they had struggled against aristocracy, they found themselves easily arrayed against the rich planters near the coast. Inasmuch as the planters in control of the seaboard slave states administered government in the interest of the slaveholding, a class to which the mountaineers did not belong, the newcomers politically opposed the planters of the lowlands and sometimes promoted the cause of abolition. It required considerable time before they could be indoctrinated in the proslavery propaganda in the proportion as slavery extended into the valley between the Blue Ridge and Allegheny Mountains, and even across the more westerly highland. This was gradually brought about, however, and before the Civil War, the small slaveholders of the upland and trans-Allegheny districts who had increased their acreage and their number of slaves grew so lukewarm on the question that abolition in those parts became unpopular and even dangerous by 1840.

If, however, as you have said, the planters of the South realized that slavery was doomed, why did they wage war for the right to perpetuate the institution? Why did they practically re-establish slavery through the vagrancy acts immediately after the Civil War in their first effort at reconstruction? And why do parts of that section still practice slavery in the form of peonage? There are in the South today intelligent white people who say that slavery was wrong, but there are few of them who do not still give unstinted praise to their leaders who fought, bled, and died for the right to perpetuate the institution.

The churches for which you make the excuse of having remained pro-slavery until insurrectionists like Nat Turner forced them the other way hardly changed their attitude altogether on account of the deeds of such men. The evangelical denominations like the Methodists and Baptists were anti-slavery in the beginning because they were not tolerated prior to the American Revolution; and, in certain parts, existed on sufferance even after religious freedom had been legally established. Slaveholders and aristocratic people in general did not as a rule belong to these churches. The Baptists and Methodists, therefore, made their appeal directly to poor whites and Negroes. Negroes were welcomed not only as communicants but even as ministers preaching to both races. As American people became further removed from the traditional attitude toward these evangelical sects, however, there was less stigma attached to membership therein; and the well-to-do began to join the ranks. Furthermore, some of the very poor whites who had at first connected with these churches became slaveholders as they developed in the economic world. This was the easiest way an employer could obtain labor in a slaveholding section. When slavery thus crept into these popular churches, therefore, the antislavery element in the congregations in the South tended to diminish until the national churches finally divided as a result of a contest during the crisis. Southern communicants had some serious fears of servile insurrection; but this was not sufficient to break the tie, for the northern churches which denounced slavery denounced also servile insurrection.

Your contention that the South would have probably granted civic rights to the Negroes and would have liberated the slaves, if it had not been for the insurrections like that of Nat Turner, cannot be proved. Uprisings like these help rather than hinder reform movements. While they may cause the lukewarm to shift from one side to another, they usually result in more sharply defining the issue and in forcing an immediate decision of the tremendously important question. The main reason for considering the emancipation of the slaves in those southern states which did not produce sugar and cotton was that slavery was becoming economically impossible. Slavery can exist in a society only when the slave can produce sufficient for himself and his master. This was gradually ceasing to be the case in the southern states which produced neither sugar nor cotton. Furthermore, because of a lack of knowledge as to fertilization and rotation of crops, the land in the declining states had been worn out. Capital from these states, then, tended to go to the more promising cotton states along the Gulf of Mexico, where young men from the declining section found it possible to retrieve their lost fortunes. The idea of emancipating slaves for this economic reason, however, soon passed from the minds of the slaveholders in the seaboard states when their problem was to some extent solved by the employment of slaves in railroad construction and in the breeding of slaves to supply the market in the lower South. Negro men and women were mated and matched for the purpose of breeding. Negro women in these selfsame states, moreover, were hired out and disposed of to lustful white men for sexual purposes; and some of these owners actually sold their own blood to supply the interstate slave trade.

The statement as to the benevolent aspect of slavery is a self-refutable contention. There were kind slaveholders who treated their slaves as human beings. But these men stood out exceptionally like shining lights after a prolonged darkness had covered the land. Some of these benevolent masters were silent abolitionists, for a few of them moved North, freed their slaves, and joined the antislavery crusade. If slavery was such an ideal situation, however, why was it necessary for the slaveholding states to maintain a patrol system for slave control and devise all sorts of laws to prevent the slaves from escaping? And why did an average of a thousand slaves a year risk their lives in making the dash for liberty across the border and into Canada? If the slaves were so much better fed and clothed and had less to do than the free laborers of the North why did not they take the places made vacant by the slaves who escaped to the North? The white laborers of the North could have come South much more easily than the slaves could go North; and the recent migration easily proves that free labor goes where it can do best in economic improvement.

You make yourself facetious in referring to such a work as *Uncle Tom's Cabin* as being untrue. This is a novel and in no sense a treatise like those referred to elsewhere in your paper. I have never heard of a literary man expressing surprise that such literature cannot be supported by documentary evidence. On such a basis the Bible itself would be condemned. *Uncle Tom's Cabin* met the test of realism. While Mrs. Stowe did not live in the South, she lived in Cincinnati right across the river where she had every opportunity to learn what was going on in slaveholding Kentucky. No single slave ever had exactly the same experience as that of Uncle Tom, but there were numbers of slaves whose hardships all but paralleled what is set forth in this narrative. The story of Josiah Henson is very much like it. George Woodson, an uncle of the undersigned, held as a slave in Fluvanna County, Virginia, went through most of such hardships. He was cruelly whipped from time to time because he would not be a good slave. He was finally beaten almost to death, then washed down in salt and water, and sold south where, like many other slaves, he was driven to death in the land of cotton.

In your treatment of the abolitionists, you seem to misunderstand reformers and reform movements. It is essential to a reformer to consider himself right and to denounce as wrong everybody else who does not agree with him. Reformers are inclined to overestimate and sometimes to exaggerate. However, you cannot produce facts to prove that as a rule the abolitionists deliberately misrepresented the situation in the South. Most of them had never lived in the South; and because of their attitude toward slavery they were not permitted to visit that section. What they had to say, therefore, was largely what they had heard or read. A story in passing from mouth to mouth may become decidedly modified without any evil intention on the part of the person who may incorporate it into a book. The antislavery leaders selected the most flagrant cases of cruelties and murders to prove that slavery was an intolerable evil; and the proslavery advocates pointed out the most benevolent acts of masters to prove that the institution was a blessing from God. Investigation, however, shows that there were many more atrocities committed in the South than the few which the abolitionists heard of and published to the world. The slaveholders did not publish their cruelties abroad, and the slaves had no means for so doing.

You refer to Philo Tower's statement as an exaggeration as to the amount of food alloted the slaves in the South. You further quote from Horace Moulton to show that the one story was taken from the other. As a matter of fact, however, both of these statements of the abolitionists with respect to food of slaves are true with some modification. I was born in Virginia and personally knew slaves of poor masters who said they did not even have as much to eat as that granted by these abolitionists. Some of their masters were so poor at times that they did not always have better diet themselves. Slaves of certain masters, moreover, were sometimes given merely a part of what they actually needed to live on, the understanding being that they would raise pigs and produce vegetables in their own gardens which they had to cultivate at night and on holidays. Sometimes it was understood, too, that they would steal a part of their food from the plantations of slaveholders who were more favorably circumstanced. I knew a white man in Buckingham County, Virginia, who was widely known as one who took care of himself and his slaves in this way.

As a rule, however, the slaves were not only given a peck or a peck and a half of corn meal a week, but were also allowed about three pounds of bacon. They were not generally supplied with vegetables as you have said. There are some plantation records of the richest and most benevolent masters showing such allowances, but these were exceptions to the rule; and the written record in this case may give only the unusual instances, inasmuch as a large majority of middle-class slaveholders never reached the point of keeping such careful records of their transactions as was done on the plantations of the few educated masters.

These provisions allowed the slaves, moreover, were not only the best they could obtain during their bondage; but even in freedom, when they were in a position to demand better food, Negro farm laborers had to content themselves with such fare. During the Nineties, the undersigned himself worked on a plantation in Virginia for twenty-five cents a day, a peck and a half of meal and three pounds of bacon a week. He worked on another plantation where he received forty cents a day but there was no allowance of vegetables. His bread was the ordinary corn pone kneaded only with salt, soda, and water and without lard. He had also a small rasher of fat bacon and sometimes a little cheap black molasses so thin that it could hardly stain the plate. Such diet is being offered today in many of the agricultural sections of the South, and Negroes still enslaved by peonage cannot better their condition or move from the plantations.

You make another error in questioning the abolitionists' contention that Negroes in the South were cruelly beaten and killed. I do not believe that you will find in abolition literature a sweeping statement that slaveholders made a business of killing Negroes. No reformer would have had such a little common sense as to think that slaveholders could have profited by their slaves if they killed them for slight offenses. But you do find evidence to the effect that Negroes were unnecessarily beaten and killed. The facts collected by any unbiased investigator in southern history will prove this. John Spencer Bassett's apology for the cruelties of slavery may have some justification in the enlightened parts of the slave states among the few liberal masters, some of whom became abolitionists. No such favorable conditions generally obtained on the large tobacco, sugar, and cotton plantations. There are thousands of witnesses to the contrary, and some of them slaveholders themselves. (See the *Diary of Landon Carter, William and Mary Quarterly Magazine,* Vol. XV, p. 150; Vol. XVI, p. 150; Fifthian's *Journal and Letters,* p. 68-69; J. H. Wynne's *General History of the British Empire in America,* p. 541; Crevecoeur's *Letters from an American Farmer,* pp. 222-224; *Abstract of the Evidence delivered before a Select Committee of the House of Commons in the Years, 1790-1791; on the Part of the Petitioners for the Abolition of the Slave Trade;* Abbé Robin's *New Travels through North America,* p. 48.)

The Negroes naturally recoiled from slavery. They had to be "broken in." To reduce them to servitude, their owners resorted to harsh measures. Some Negroes never yielded altogether to these corrective measures. If they did not submit, the masters considered them better off when dead, for the owners could not support them in the capacity of free men from whom no profit could be derived. I have personally talked with hundreds of slaves who passed through the ordeals which are in no sense exaggerated by most of these abolition treatises which you question. I do think that the slaves who felt the lash upon their backs and saw their fellow men killed should be permitted to testify in their own behalf, even if you do rule out of court the abolitionists who were the only persons who had the moral courage to speak out in their behalf. The victims of the lash knew more about these cruelties than post bellum observers.

Furthermore, there are court records which prove that masters were punished for cruelly beating and killing slaves. (See B. T. Catterall's *Judicial Cases concerning American Slavery and the Negro,* pp. 94, 113, 118, 128, 131, 150, 174, 181, 182, 186, 187, 208, 223-225, 235, 290, 296, 298, 299, 304, 308, 309, 312, 322, 323, 325, 328, 331, 341, 347, 380, 385, 390, 402, 404, 408, 409, 410, 422, 423, 425,

442.) These court records, restricted to Virginia, West Virginia, and Kentucky where slavery existed in a milder form than in the lower South, moreover, show cases of the killing of Negroes by being "fired upon by patrols," "through abuse under hire," "by exposure," and "by cruel and excessive punishment." The cases adjudicated were evidently a small fraction of such offenses; for, as in the case of Virginia, states had positive laws exonerating masters from punishment of their slaves and even from killing them in the act if the offender could hide behind the pretext of resistance or accident. (See 2 *Hening* 270 and 12 *Hening* 681. See also St. George Tucker's *A Dissertation on Slavery,* pp. 50-51; A. P. Scott's *History of Criminal Law in Colonial Virginia,* pp. 232-234, in manuscript form at the University of Chicago; *The Virginia Magazine of History and Biography,* Vol. XII, p. 437; *The Official Letters of Alexander Spottswood, Collections of the Virginia Historical Society,* Vol. II, p. 202; James Franklin's *Philosophical and Political History of the Thirteen United States of America,* p. 90; and Peter Kalm's *Travels into North America,* p. 501.)

Furthermore, your unwarranted indictment of the abolitionists is based upon a few quotations which may or may not express the truth. Quoting from practically unknown abolitionists, moreover, you have omitted from the discussion those men and women whose names come first to the mind of the historian when he mentions abolitionists. Few persons have read about Philo Tower and Horace Moulton. You have done well to mention William E. Channing and the Grimké sisters. When an historian thinks of abolitionists there come to his mind such names as those of William Lloyd Garrison, Arthur Tappan, Lewis Tappan, Wendell Phillips, Abbey Kelley Foster, Stephen S. Foster, Lucy Stone, Samuel J. May, Maria Weston Chapman, Charles F. Hovey, Eliza Lee Follen, Sydney Howard Gay, William J. Bowditch, Edmund Quincy, Nathaniel P. Rogers, Lydia Maria Child, Thomas Garrett, Susan B. Anthony, Prudence Crandall, Lunsford Lane, William Wells Brown, Charles Lenox Remond, Sojourner Truth, Frederick Douglass, Benjamin Lundy, Daniel R. Goodloe, Charles Sumner, Henry Ward Beecher, James G. Birney, Elijah Lovejoy, John G. Fee, Cassius M. Clay, Calvin Fairbank, Ruben Crandall, Theodore F. Weld, Asa Mahan, John Morgan, and Charles T. Torrey.

You should know that at times the conflict was largely a war of words. The proslavery and the antislavery elements were drawn up in battle array. The atmosphere was charged with vituperation and recrimination. Protagonists on both sides spoke without authority. Without making adequate investigation men wrote of what they had heard. Some abolitionists most assuredly made utterances which cannot be substantiated, and so did numerous proslavery advocates who falsely contended that the slaves were happily situated. The real historian would consider the errors of both sides. To infer that abolitionists were especially untruthful can result only from that bias which finds more honesty in the exploiter than in the opponent of the exploitation, more virtue in the oppressor than in the friend of the oppressed, and more sense of justice in the slaveholder than in the martyr to freedom. We have suffered from considerable moral degeneracy, but the majority of the American people has hardly descended to such a depth of so distorting the truth.

Propaganda writers are accustomed to refer to the abolitionists as unusually excited persons who by their radicalism did the cause of freedom more harm than good. These authors contend that slavery would have eventually come to an end as a result of the logical arraignment of it through spokesmen of southern poor whites and northern free laborers, but the abolitionists, climaxing their efforts with such uprisings as those of Nat Turner and John Brown, precipitated the Civil War. Writers of this type, however, manifest just about as much reason as the man who, finding his friend decided to have an incurably diseased limb amputated, advised him not to undergo such a painful operation because the limb would eventually rot off. The work of Abraham Lincoln would have been impossible if he had not been preceded by the abolitionists. In the crisis he had to come to the position of instant abolition, for his plan was to get rid of the institution through gradual and compensated emancipation by 1900. The conflict of the antislavery and proslavery forces became inevitable. The abolitionists kept the question before the country. They actually excited the South and forced it to the position of militantly defending medievalism. The moral and spiritual cost of the conflict which ensued was tremendous, but it had to come. History shows that the human family is still too spiritually weak to work out such problems by peaceful means.

To undertake to discredit the unselfish work of the abolitionists exhibits a rather unfortunate state of mind. To ignore the record of these men and women of vision would be merely omitting a most interesting part of our history. These reformers worked jointly for temperance, legal reform, woman suffrage, and the rights of labor. If you eliminate their record, then, our history will become an artless tale which few will care to read. People will not eternally delight in the vices, follies, and quarrels of those who contend for power to oppress the weak. The public will not always recite the exploits of the oppressor nor idolize the man who "wrings his bread from the sweat of another's brow." We shall some day appreciate these reformers who were so far ahead of their time. They endeavored to lift man above selfishness unto an altruism of a regenerated universe. They labored to realize the ideals for which Socrates, Jesus Christ, and John Brown died. Following the examples of the martyrs of old, some of these idealists even gave their lives as a sacrifice for freedom. They lived up to the ideal of the Great Nazarene who said: "Greater love hath no man than this, that a man lay down his life for his friends."

Respectfully yours,

C. G. Woodson

Langston Hughes

Among the most articulate of the race-conscious poets and essayists of the Harlem Renaissance and the Negro revolution of the 1960's is (James) Langston Hughes (1902-—). He was born in Joplin, Missouri, of mixed ancestry which included French and Indian forebears. One ancestor, he liked to point out, was a companion of John Brown. His divorced mother raised him as a child in Lawrence, Kansas, and after she remarried she sent Langston to a Cleveland high school where he wrote poems about the steel mills where his stepfather worked, the encompassing slums, and the brown girls from the South. During his Harlem days, he attended Columbia University and he describes these exhilarating years below. In his footloose life, he wandered along Italy's shores as a beachcomber. In 1929, Lincoln University awarded him his B.A., and as his literary reputation grew, the University of Chicago made him poet-in-residence in 1949; in 1964, Western Reserve University honored him as Doctor of Letters.

Out of his Harlem world came his first book, *The Weary Blues* (1926), poems that expressed the exoticism of that era. His prize-winning novel, *Not Without Laughter* (1930), tells the story of Negro youth. During the Depression he fused his race consciousness with economic protest. During the Spanish Civil War he covered the Loyalist cause for the *Baltimore Afro-American* and wrote a column for the *Chicago Defender*.

He has been a prolific writer of short stories, poems, plays, anthologies, and autobiographies. "My Early Days in Harlem" is a condensation of other writings on the literary renaissance of the 1920's and is reprinted with his permission. It appeared in *Freedomways,* III (1963), pp. 312-314. His autobiography, *I Wonder as I Wander* (New York: Holt, Rinehart & Winston, 1956), pp. 50-54 is excerpted for a striking incident of 1931 and is reprinted with the permission of Langston Hughes, Hill and Wang, Inc., and Harold Ober Associates, Inc. Copyright © 1956 by Langston Hughes.

My Early Days in Harlem

On a bright September morning in 1921, I came up out of the subway at 135th and Lenox into the beginnings of the Negro Renaissance. I headed for the Harlem Y.M.C.A. down the block, where so many new, young, dark, male arrivals in Harlem have spent early days. The next place I headed to that afternoon was the Harlem Branch Library just up the street. There, a warm and wonderful librarian, Miss Ernestine Rose, white, made newcomers feel welcome, as did her assistant in charge of the Schomburg Collection, Catherine Latimer, a luscious café au lait. That night I went to the Lincoln Theatre across Lenox Avenue where maybe one of the Smiths—Bessie, Clara, Trixie, or Mamie—was singing the blues. And as soon as I could, I made a beeline for *Shuffle Along,* the all-colored hit musical playing on 63rd Street in which Florence Mills came to fame.

I had come to New York to enter Columbia College as a freshman, but *really* why I had come to New York was to see Harlem. I found it hard a week or so later to tear myself away from Harlem when it came time to move up the hill to the dormitory at Columbia. That winter I spent as little time as possible on the campus. Instead, I spent as much time as I could in Harlem, and this I have done ever since. I was in love with Harlem long before I got there, and I still am in love with it. Everybody seemed to make me welcome. The sheer dark size of Harlem intrigued me. And the fact that at that time poets and writers like James Weldon Johnson and Jessie Fauset lived there, and Bert Williams, Duke Ellington, Ethel Waters, and Walter White, too, fascinated me. Had I been a rich young man, I would have bought a house in Harlem and built musical steps up to the front door, and installed chimes that at the press of a button played Ellington tunes.

After a winter at Columbia, I moved back down to Harlem.

Everywhere I roomed, I had the good fortune to have lovely landladies. If I did not like a landlady's looks, I would not move in with her, maybe that is why. But at finding work in New York, my fortune was less than good. Finally, I went to sea—Africa, Europe—then a year in Paris working in a night club where the band was from Harlem. I was a dishwasher, later bus boy, listening every night to the music of Harlem transplanted to Montmartre. And I was on hand to welcome Bricktop when she came to sing for the first time in Europe, bringing with her news of Harlem.

When I came back to New York in 1925 the Negro Renaissance was in full swing. Countee Cullen was publishing his early poems, Aaron Douglas was painting, Zora Neale Hurston, Rudolph Fisher, Jean Toomer, and Wallace Thurman were writing, Louis Armstrong was playing, Cora La Redd was dancing, and the Savoy Ballroom was open with a specially built floor that rocked as the dancers swayed. Alain Locke was putting together *The New Negro*. Art took heart from Harlem creativity. Jazz filled the night air—but not everywhere—and people came from all around after dark to look upon our city within a city, Black Harlem. Had I not had to earn a living, I might have thought it even more wonderful than it was. But I could not eat the poems I wrote. Unlike the whites who came to spend their money in Harlem, only a few Harlemites seemed to live in even a modest degree of luxury. Most rode the subway downtown every morning to work or to look for work.

Downtown! I soon learned that it was seemingly impossible for black Harlem to live without white downtown. My youthful illusion that Harlem was a world unto itself did not last very long. It was not even an area that ran itself. The famous night clubs were owned by whites, as were the theaters. Almost all the stores were owned by whites, and many at that time did not even (in the very middle of Harlem) employ Negro clerks. The books of Harlem writers all had to be published downtown, if they were to be published at all. Downtown: *white*. Uptown: *black*. White downtown pulling all the strings in Harlem. Moe Gale, Moe Gale, Moe Gale, Lew Leslie, Lew Leslie, Lew Leslie, Harper's, Knopf, *The Survey Graphic,* the Harmon Foundation, the racketeers who kidnapped Casper Holstein and began to take over the numbers for whites. Negroes could not even play their own numbers with their *own* people. And almost all the policemen in Harlem were white. Negroes couldn't even get graft from *themselves* for themselves by themselves. Black Harlem really was in white face, economically speaking. So I wrote this poem:

Because my mouth
Is wide with laughter
And my throat
Is deep with song,
You do not think
I suffer after
I have held my pain
So long?
Because my mouth
Is wide with laughter,
You do not hear
My inner cry?
Because my feet
Are gay with dancing,
You do not know
I die?

Harlem, like a Picasso painting in his cubistic period. Harlem—southern Harlem—the Carolinas, Georgia, Florida—looking for the Promised Land—dressed in rhythmic words, painted in bright pictures, dancing to jazz—and ending up in the subway at morning rush time—*headed downtown.* West Indian Harlem—warm rambunctious sassy remembering Marcus Garvey. Haitian Harlem, Cuban Harlem, little pockets of tropical dreams in alien tongues. Magnet Harlem, pulling an Arthur Schomburg from Puerto Rico, pulling an Arna Bontemps all the way from California, a Nora Holt from way out West, an E. Simms Campbell from St. Louis, likewise a Josephine Baker, a Charles S. Johnson from Virginia, an A. Philip Randolph from Florida, a Roy Wilkins from Minnesota, an Alta Douglas from Kansas. Melting pot Harlem—Harlem of honey and chocolate and caramel and rum and vinegar and lemon and lime and gall. Dusky dream Harlem rumbling into a nightmare tunnel where the subway from the Bronx keeps right on downtown, where the money from the nightclubs goes right on back downtown, where the jazz is drained to Broadway, whence Josephine goes to Paris, Robeson to London, Jean Toomer to a Quaker Meeting House, Garvey to the Atlanta Federal Penitentiary, and Wallace Thurman to his grave; but Duke Ellington to fame and fortune, Lena Horne to Broadway, and Buck Clayton to China.

Before it was over—our New Negro Renaissance—poems became placards: DON'T BUY WHERE YOU CAN'T WORK! Adam Powell with a picket sign; me, too. BUY BLACK! Sufi long before the Black Muslims. FIRST TO BE FIRED, LAST TO BE HIRED! The Stock Market crash. The bank failures. Empty pockets. *God Bless The Child That's Got His Own*. Depression. Federal Theater in Harlem, the making of Orson Welles. WPA, CCC, the Blue Eagle, Father Divine. In the midst of the Depression I got a cable from Russia inviting me to work on a motion picture there. I went to Moscow. That was the end of the early days of Langston Hughes in Harlem.

I Wonder as I Wander

Warning in Mississippi

On the Sunday afternoon when I read my poems at Bethune-Cookman College with Mary McLeod Bethune presiding, I closed with "The Negro Mother" from my new booklet. "Imagine," I said, "a black woman of old in her starched white apron and bright bandanna."

"My son, my son!" cried Mrs. Bethune, rising with tears in her eyes to embrace me on the platform. In closing, her choir sang, "We Are Climbing Jacob's Ladder," as the largely white audience of winter visitors from the big Daytona Beach hotels filled the baskets with checks and greenbacks.

Mrs. Bethune knew how to get things done. She once told me, "People wonder how I can move into action these poor colored women's clubs in some of our backward towns, get them building their own clubhouses and community centers and setting up libraries, and doing something else besides just meeting and eating. Well, when I am presiding over a district meeting, I simply tell these women what I want done. I say, 'Now, I want Sister So-and-So to make a motion to do this, that or the other thing, whatever it is. . . . Now, I want you, Sister, over there to second this motion. . . . Now I want everybody here—I said *everybody*—to vote, *Aye!*—Let's vote. . . . Motion carried.' "

In Miami, I gave a program in an undertaker's parlor, since Negroes had no auditorium there. Then from Florida we drove along the Gulf to New Orleans where I was presented at Straight College. After the program a teen-age girl came up to me with a sheaf of poems, which I glanced at quickly, between shaking hands and autographing books that Raddie was selling. I took the poems to be the usual poor output so often thrust into my hands at public gatherings. Then, almost immediately, I saw that these poems showed talent, so I spent an hour after the program going over them with the girl and pointing out to her where I thought they might be improved. The youngster's name was Margaret Walker. A dozen years later her first book of poems, *For My People,* received the Yale University Younger Poets Award. The author sent me an advance copy inscribed:

To Langston—in gratitude
for his encouragement even
when the poems were no good.
Sincerely,
Margaret Walker

Southern University on the Mississippi near Baton Rouge, with its charming old campus beneath the live oaks and hanging moss, was our next stop. Then into the State of Mississippi, to Jackson, Piney Woods, Holly Springs, and Meridian. At Meridian a kindly old white gentleman in the audience came up and said gently, "I just want to warn you that you shouldn't be reading those race-equality poems in Meridian, and you'd better be careful selling your books. There are folks in this state who wouldn't like what you say."

I knew that there were towns in Mississippi where Negro newspapers from the North were not allowed to be sold openly. Vendors had to bootleg Negro papers containing democracy-for-all editorials, and one man I'd met had been run out of town for selling *The Chicago Defender*. Mississippi was a state where few Negroes then dared to vote for fear of violence. In that year, 1931, there had been twelve lynchings in the South. Several of my poems were about voting and lynching; and I always read some of them on each program, as well as one or two poems about the Scottsboro Case. It was my poetry of this type which caused the kindly old white man to warn me about his fellow Mississippians. But, in contrast, at Greenville, Mississippi, in the very heart of the levee country, the leading white poet of the state, Will Alexander Percy, acted as the chairman of my program at a Negro church. He introduced me most graciously to the audience. Later he sent me an inscribed copy of his autobiography, *Lanterns on the Levee,* and over the years that followed I had several beautiful letters from him. But I met less than half a dozen such gentlemanly Southerners on my winter-long tour. Instead, I found a great social and cultural gulf between the races in the South, astonishing to one who, like myself, from the North, had never known such uncompromising prejudices. Of course, a Negro traveler soon got accustomed to—even if never able to accept emotionally—the many visible evidences of legal segregation: the WHITE and COLORED signs everywhere from station waiting rooms to public water fountains, the Jim Crow cars on the trains, the COLORED ENTRANCE placards in the alleys where movie stairways led up to the highest gallery, the restaurants where Negroes could not eat, and so on. But the unpredictable and unexpected things that suddenly happened are the things I never forget.

Once I was late for an evening engagement because, at a river crossing where the bridge was under repair, a ferry was being used. But all the Negro cars on the road had to wait until *all* the white cars in line, no matter how far back, had gotten on the boat. The ferry captain would fill his boat up with white automobiles and leave the Negro cars standing there. By the time the boat crossed the river and came back, more white drivers had gathered. The ferry master would again motion the whites onto the boat ahead of the Negroes. Finally I was allowed to get across the river.

A less irritating but more fantastic incident happened in Savannah. In New York every Sunday, due especially to my interest in the *Book Review* section, I always bought the *Times*. It was not always easy to find a Sunday *Times* in the South. But whenever I stopped in a large city, I tried to find it.

In Savannah I learned that the *Times* might be purchased at a newsstand in one of the railway stations, so I walked down to the station one afternoon to secure a copy. In the colored waiting room there was no newsstand, so I went outside on the sidewalk and around into the white waiting room where I bought the *Sunday Times* without incident. But, coming out of the station, just at the door, a white policeman stopped me.

He yelled, "You can't come in and out this door."

"There's no newsstand in the colored waiting room," I explained.

"I don't care nothing about that!" he barked. "You can't come in this door. This is for white folks."

"Oh," I said, "I am going out now."

"You can't go out this way neither," said the cop as I started through the door.

This puzzled me, as there was no other way out of the station except through the train sheds. "I just came in this way," I said.

"Well, you can't go out this way," barked the cop. "Niggers can't use this door."

"How do I get out then?" I asked.

"Only way I see," said the cop seriously, "is for you to walk the tracks."

In order to get out of the Savannah station with the *New York Times* that day, I had to go through the train gates and follow the railroad tracks to the nearest crossing to reach the street. I had never experienced anything so absurd before. The seriousness of that white policeman and the utter stupidity of being *at* a door, but not permitted to go *through* it, made me burst out laughing as I walked along with my paper from Manhattan.

I remembered, when I was in my teens, coming up from a summer in Mexico on my return to school in Cleveland, I had gone into the dining car one evening as the train was heading through Texas. I was seated alone when a white man came in. Without looking, he sat down opposite me. When I glanced across the table, I saw that the man was staring at me with a look of utter amazement. Suddenly the man jumped as though he had been shot and cried, "Why, you're a nigger, ain't you?" Then the man fled from the dining car as though he had sat down in front of a lion by mistake. As many Negroes as there are in Texas, what could there be about just *one* at a table in a public dining car that could so startle a white man? The colored waiters who saw the incident laughed, and so did I.

This was the sort of thing that continually puzzled and amused me in the South. Certainly the much lauded Southern gentility and aristocratic good manners are seldom shown toward Negroes. . . . The Savannah policeman did not say, "Sir, I am sorry, but you are in the wrong place." He simply barked, "You can't come in here!" When I thought about these things seriously, they were not funny. They were boorish and stupid. Some years later when I asked Carson McCullers, the Georgia writer, why white people in the South behaved so badly toward Negroes, Mrs. McCullers said, "Their hind brains don't work."

Richard Wright

Actually, few of the militant Negro intellectuals crossed over into the Communist camp, although it became fashionable to talk like fellow-travelers during the Great Depression. Even Du Bois flatly rejected Communism in 1931 and proclaimed himself a member only at ninety-three. Richard Wright (1908-1960), who did join the party (as the selection indicates), wrote an emphatic recantation. The Communists argued that Negroes had nothing to lose by uniting with Moscow and offered "self-determination for the Black Belt" with a Negro vice-presidential nominee in James Ford, but they aroused little response.

Dr. Du Bois published a revealing article, "The Negro and Communism," in his NAACP journal, *The Crisis,* in September, 1931, which offered an explanation of why Negroes rejected Communism and voted with middle-class whites against the "demagogues" of the South and their lower-class supporters:

> The persons who are killing blacks in northern Alabama are the white workers—sharecroppers, trade unionists, and artisans. The capitalists are against mob law and violence and would listen to justice in the long run because industrial peace increases their profits. On the other hand, the white workers want to kill the competition of "Niggers." Thereupon, the Communists, seizing leadership of the poorest and most ignorant blacks, head them towards slaughter and jailslavery, while they hide safely in Chattanooga and Harlem.

Thus Du Bois could make a class-oriented analysis of politics and conclude with an anti-Communist observation. And southern Negro voters continued as in Bourbon times to vote for middle-class candidates. (See "Race Relations and Class Structures," by Walter B. Simon in *The Journal of Social Psychology,* Vol. 60 (1963), 187-193.)

Richard Wright was born on a Mississippi plantation near Natchez on September 4, 1908, the son of a mill-worker and a schoolteacher. Neglected as a youth, he was raised by kinfolk, educated only sporadically despite his obviously acute mind, and then plunged into a delinquent-breeding environment. He tramped to Memphis and other cities, worked as a porter, bell-boy, ditch-digger, and clerk. In Chicago, he made some progress as a political campaign worker but when he was denied a promised job, he angrily joined the Communist party.

By 1935 his evident talents enabled him to begin a productive literary career on the Federal Writers' Project in Chicago during which he published poetry, stories, and essays in various magazines. His short stories that dealt with violent racial frustrations appeared in *Uncle Tom's Children*. A Guggenheim Fellowship helped him to complete his important novel *Native Son* (1940), which became a Book of the Month selection. This novel combined his favorite theme of the Negro lost in a white man's world and the then popular environmentalist philosophy of *Dead End*. He told of the brutal murder of a kindly white woman by a pathological Negro youth, Bigger Thomas, who came out of Chicago's rat-infested South Side Negro tenements, where Negro youths daydreamed about opportunities reserved only for whites. The most engaging character is the Communist defense lawyer at the trial who presents a left-wing interpretation of the tragedy. Critics praised Wright's honesty and authentic reportorial style. His frightening naturalism far exceeded in intensity the much more restrained realism or primitivism of Julia Peterkin, Du Bose Heyward, and Paul Green, who had "discovered" the Negro during the 1920's.

This selection is Richard Wright's confessional essay in Richard Crossman, ed., *The God That Failed* (New York: Harper & Row, Publishers, Inc., 1944), pp. 150-162. Copyright 1944 by Richard Wright. It illustrates Wright's final rebellion against Communist thought control and the uncomfortable reaction of fellow Negroes to Communism. Reprinted by permission of Harper & Row, Publishers, Inc.

From *The God That Failed*

I was transferred by the relief authorities from the South Side Boys' Club to the Federal Negro Theater to work as a publicity agent. There were days when I was acutely hungry for the incessant analyses that went on among the comrades, but whenever I heard news of the party's inner life, it was of charges and countercharges, reprisals and counter-reprisals.

The Federal Negro Theater, for which I was doing publicity, had run a series of ordinary plays, all of which had been revamped to "Negro style," with jungle scenes, spirituals, and all. For example, the skinny white woman who directed it, an elderly missionary type, would take a play whose characters were white, whose theme dealt with the Middle Ages, and recast it in terms of Southern Negro life with overtones of African backgrounds. Contemporary plays dealing realistically with Negro life were spurned as being controversial. There were about forty Negro actors and actresses in the theater, lolling about, yearning, disgruntled.

What a waste of talent, I thought. Here was an opportunity for the production of a worth-while Negro drama and no one was aware of it. I studied the situation, then laid the matter before white friends of mine who held influential positions in the Works Progress Administration. I asked them to replace the white woman—including her quaint aesthetic notions—with someone who knew the Negro and the theater. They promised me that they would act.

Within a month the white woman director had been transferred. We moved from the South Side to the Loop and were housed in a first-rate theater. I successfully recommended Charles DeSheim, a talented Jew, as director. DeSheim and I held long talks during which I outlined what I thought could be accomplished. I urged that our first offering should be a bill of three one-act plays, including Paul Green's *Hymn to the Rising Sun,* a grim, poetical, powerful one-acter dealing with chain-gang conditions in the South.

I was happy. At last I was in a position to make suggestions and have them acted upon. I was convinced that we had a rare chance to build a genuine Negro theater. I convoked a meeting and introduced DeSheim to the Negro company, telling them that he was a man who knew the theater, who would lead them toward serious dramatics. DeSheim made a speech wherein he said that he was not at the theater to direct it, but to help the Negroes to direct it. He spoke so simply and eloquently that they rose and applauded him.

I then proudly passed out copies of Paul Green's *Hymn to the*

Rising Sun to all members of the company. DeSheim assigned reading parts. I sat down to enjoy adult Negro dramatics. But something went wrong. The Negroes stammered and faltered in their lines. Finally they stopped reading altogether. DeSheim looked frightened. One of the Negro actors rose.

"Mr. DeSheim," he began, "we think this play is indecent. We don't want to act in a play like this before the American public. I don't think any such conditions exist in the South. I lived in the South and I never saw any chain gangs. Mr. DeSheim, we want a play that will make the public love us."

"What kind of play do you want?" DeSheim asked them.

They did not know. I went to the office and looked up their records and found that most of them had spent their lives playing cheap vaudeville because the legitimate theater was barred to them, and now it turned out they wanted none of the legitimate theater, that they were scared spitless at the prospects of appearing in a play that the public might not like, even though they did not understand that public and had no way of determining its likes or dislikes.

I felt—but only temporarily—that perhaps the whites were right, that Negroes were children and would never grow up. DeSheim informed the company that he would produce any play they liked, and they sat like frightened mice, possessing no words to make known their vague desires.

When I arrived at the theater a few mornings later, I was horrified to find that the company had drawn up a petition demanding the ousting of DeSheim. I was asked to sign the petition and I refused.

"Don't you know your friends?" I asked them.

They glared at me. I called DeSheim to the theater and we went into a frantic conference.

"What must I do?" he asked.

"Take them into your confidence," I said. "Let them know that it is their right to petition for a redress of their grievances."

DeSheim thought my advice sound and, accordingly, he assembled the company and told them that they had a right to petition against him if they wanted to, but that he thought any misunderstandings that existed could be settled smoothly.

"Who told you that we were getting up a petition?" a black man demanded.

DeSheim looked at me and stammered wordlessly.

"There's an Uncle Tom in the theater!" a black girl yelled.

After the meeting a delegation of Negro men came to my office and took out their pocketknives and flashed them in my face.

"You get the hell off this job before we cut your bellybutton out!" they said.

I telephoned my white friends in the Works Progress Administration: "Transfer me at once to another job, or I'll be murdered."

Within twenty-four hours DeSheim and I were given our papers. We shook hands and went our separate ways.

I was transferred to a white experimental theatrical company as a publicity agent and I resolved to keep my ideas to myself, or, better, to write them down and not attempt to translate them into reality.

One evening a group of Negro Communists called at my home and asked to speak to me in strict secrecy. I took them into my room and locked the door.

"Dick," they began abruptly, "the party wants you to attend a meeting Sunday."

"Why?" I asked. "I'm no longer a member."

"That's all right. They want you to be present," they said.

"Communists don't speak to me on the street," I said. "Now, why do you want me at a meeting?"

They hedged. They did not want to tell me.

"If you can't tell me, then I can't come," I said.

They whispered among themselves and finally decided to take me into their confidence.

"Dick, Ross is going to be tried," they said.

"For what?"

They recited a long list of political offenses of which they alleged that he was guilty.

"But what has that got to do with me?"

"If you come, you'll find out," they said.

"I'm not that naïve," I said. I was suspicious now. Were they trying to lure me to a trial and expel me? "This trial might turn out to be mine."

They swore that they had no intention of placing me on trial, that the party merely wanted me to observe Ross's trial so that I might learn what happened to "enemies of the working class."

As they talked, my old love of witnessing something new came over me. I wanted to see this trial, but I did not want to risk being placed on trial myself.

"Listen," I told them. "I'm not guilty of Nealson's charges. If I showed up at this trial, it would seem that I am."

"No, it won't. Please come."

"All right. But, listen, If I'm tricked, I'll fight. You hear? I don't trust Nealson. I'm not a politician and I cannot anticipate all the funny moves of a man who spends his waking hours plotting."

Ross's trial took place that following Sunday afternoon. Comrades stood inconspicuously on guard about the meeting hall, at the doors, down the street, and along the hallways. When I appeared, I was ushered in quickly. I was tense. It was a rule that once you had entered a meeting of this kind you could not leave until the meeting was over; it was feared that you might go to the police and denounce them all.

Ross, the accused, sat alone at a table in the front of the hall, his face distraught. I felt sorry for him; yet I could not escape feeling that he enjoyed this. For him, this was perhaps the highlight of an otherwise bleak existence.

In trying to grasp why Communists hated intellectuals, my mind was led back again to the accounts I had read of the Russian Revolution. There had existed in Old Russia millions of poor, ignorant people who were exploited by a few educated, arrogant noblemen, and it became natural for the Russian Communists to associate betrayal with intellectualism. But there existed in the Western world an element that baffled and frightened the Communist party: the prevalence of self-achieved literacy. Even a Negro, entrapped by ignorance and exploitation—as I had been—could, if he had the will and the love for it, learn to read and understand the world in which he lived. And it was these people that the Communists could not understand.

The trial began in a quiet, informal manner. The comrades acted like a group of neighbors sitting in judgment upon one of their kind who had stolen a chicken. Anybody could ask and get the floor. There was absolute freedom of speech. Yet the meeting had an amazingly formal structure of its own, a structure that went as deep as the desire of men to live together.

A member of the Central Committee of the Communist Party rose and gave a description of the world situation. He spoke without emotion and piled up hard facts. He painted a horrible but masterful picture of Fascism's aggression in Germany, Italy, and Japan.

I accepted the reason why the trial began in this manner. It was imperative that here be postulated against what or whom Ross's crimes had been committed. Therefore there had to be established in the minds of all present a vivid picture of mankind under oppression. And it was a true picture. Perhaps no organization on earth, save the Communist party, possesses so detailed a knowledge of how workers lived, for its sources of information stemmed directly from the workers themselves.

The next speaker discussed the role of the Soviet Union as the world's lone workers' state—how the Soviet Union was hemmed in by enemies, how the Soviet Union was trying to industrialize itself, what sacrifices it was making to help workers of the world to steer a path toward peace through the idea of collective security.

The facts presented so far were as true as any facts could be in this uncertain world. Yet not one word had been said of the accused, who sat listening like any other member. The time had not yet come to include him and his crimes in this picture of global struggle. An absolute had first to be established in the minds of the comrades so that they could measure the success or failure of their deeds by it.

Finally a speaker came forward and spoke of Chicago's South Side, its Negro population, their suffering and handicaps, linking all that also to the world struggle. Then still another speaker followed and described the tasks of the Communist party of the South Side. At last, the world, the national, and the local pictures had been fused into one overwhelming drama of moral struggle in which everybody in the hall was participating. This presentation had lasted for more than three hours, but it had enthroned a new sense of reality in the hearts of those present, a sense of man on earth. With the exception of the church and its myths and legends, there was no agency in the world so capable of making men feel the earth and the people upon it as the Communist party.

Toward evening the direct charges against Ross were made, not by the leaders of the party, but by Ross's friends, those who knew him best! It was crushing. Ross wilted. His emotions could not withstand the weight of the moral pressure. No one was terrorized into giving information against him. They gave it willingly, citing dates, conversations, scenes. The black mass of Ross's wrongdoing emerged slowly and irrefutably.

The moment came for Ross to defend himself. I had been told that he had arranged for friends to testify in his behalf, but he called upon no one. He stood, trembling; he tried to talk and his words would not come. The hall was as still as death. Guilt was written in every pore of his black skin. His hands shook. He held on to the edge of the table to keep on his feet. His personality, his sense of himself, had been obliterated. Yet he could not have been so humbled unless he had shared and accepted the vision that had crushed him, the common vision that bound us all together.

"Comrades," he said in a low, charged voice, "I'm guilty of all the charges, all of them."

His voice broke in a sob. No one prodded him. No one tortured him. No one threatened him. He was free to go out of the hall and never see another Communist. But he did not want to. He could not. The vision of a communal world had sunk down into his soul and it would never leave him until life left him. He talked on, outlining how he had erred, how he would reform.

I knew, as I sat there, that there were many people who thought they knew life who had been skeptical of the Moscow trials. But they could not have been skeptical had they witnessed this astonishing trial. Ross had not been doped; he had been awakened. It was not a fear of the Communist party that had made him confess, but a fear of the punishment that he would exact of himself that made him tell of his wrongdoings. The Communists had talked to him until they had given him new eyes with which to see his own crime. And then they sat back and listened to him tell how he had erred.

He was one with all the members there, regardless of race or color; his heart was theirs and their hearts were his; and when a man reaches that state of kinship with others, that degree of oneness, or when a trial has made him kin after he has been sundered from them by wrongdoing, then he must rise and say, out of a sense of the deepest morality in the world: "I'm guilty. Forgive me."

This, to me, was a spectacle of glory; and yet, because it had condemned me, because it was blind and ignorant, I felt that it was a spectacle of horror. The blindness of their limited lives—lives truncated and impoverished by the oppression they had suffered long before they had ever heard of Communism—made them think that I was with their enemies. American life had so corrupted their consciousness that they were unable to recognize their friends when they saw them. I knew that if they had held state power I should have been declared guilty of treason and my execution would have followed. And I knew that they felt, with all the strength of their black blindness, that they were right.

I could not stay until the end. I was anxious to get out of the hall and into the streets and shake free from the gigantic tension that had hold of me. I rose and went to the door; a comrade shook his head, warning me that I could not leave until the trial had ended.

"You can't leave now," he said.

"I'm going out of here," I said, my anger making my voice louder than I intended.

We glared at each other. Another comrade came running up. I stepped forward. The comrade who had rushed up gave the signal for me to be allowed to leave. They did not want violence, and neither did I. They stepped aside.

I went into the dark Chicago streets and walked home through the cold, filled with a sense of sadness. Once again I told myself that I must learn to stand alone. I did not feel so wounded by their rejection of me that I wanted to spend my days bleating about what they had done. Perhaps what I had already learned to feel in my childhood saved me from that futile path. I lay in bed that night and said to myself: "I'll be for them, even though they are not for me."

From the Federal Experimental Theater I was transferred to the Federal Writers' Project, and I tried to earn my bread by writing guidebooks. Many of the writers on the project were members of the Communist party and they kept their revolutionary vows that restrained them from speaking to "traitors of the working class." I sat beside them in the office, ate next to them in restaurants, and rode up and down in the elevators with them, but they always looked straight ahead, wordlessly.

After working on the project for a few months, I was made acting supervisor of essays and straightway I ran into political difficulties. One morning the administrator of the project called me into his office.

"Wright, who are your friends on this project?" he asked.

"I don't know," I said. "Why?"

"Well, you ought to find out soon," he said.

"What do you mean?"

"Some people are asking for your removal on the ground that you are incompetent," he said.

"Who are they?"

He named several of my erstwhile comrades. Yes, it had come to that. They were trying to take the bread out of my mouth.

"What do you propose to do about their complaints?" I asked.

"Nothing," he said, laughing. "I think I understand what's happening here. I'm not going to let them drive you off this job."

I thanked him and rose to go to the door. Something in his words had not sounded right. I turned and faced him.

"*This* job?" I repeated. "What do you mean?"

"You mean to say that you don't know?" he asked.

"Know what? What are you talking about?"

"Why did you leave the Federal Negro Theater?"

"I had trouble there. They drove me off the job, the Negroes did."

"And you don't think that they had any encouragement?" he asked me ironically.

I sat again. This was deadly. I gaped at him.

"You needn't fear here," he said. "You work, write."

"It's hard to believe that," I murmured.

"Forget it," he said.

But the worst was yet to come. One day at noon I closed my desk and went down in the elevator. When I reached the first floor of the building, I saw a picket line moving to and fro in the streets. Many of the men and women carrying placards were old friends of mine, and they were chanting for higher wages for Works Progress Administration artists and writers. It was not the kind of picket line that one was not supposed to cross, and as I started away from the door I heard my name shouted:

"There's Wright, that goddamn Trotskyite!"

"We know you, you—!"

"Wright's a traitor!"

For a moment it seemed that I ceased to live. I had now reached that point where I was cursed aloud in the busy streets of America's second-largest city. It shook me as nothing else had.

Days passed. I continued on my job, where I functioned as the shop chairman of the union which I had helped to organize, though my election as shop chairman had been bitterly opposed by the party. In their efforts to nullify my influence in the union, my old comrades were willing to kill the union itself.

As May Day of 1936 approached, it was voted by the union membership that we should march in the public procession. On the morning of May Day I received printed instructions as to the time and place where our union contingent would assemble to join the parade. At noon, I hurried to the spot and found that the parade was already in progress. In vain I searched for the banners of my union local. Where were they? I went up and down the streets, asking for the location of my local.

"Oh, that local's gone fifteen minutes ago," a Negro told me. "If you're going to march, you'd better fall in somewhere."

I thanked him and walked through the milling crowds. Suddenly I heard my name called. I turned. To my left was the Communist party's South Side section, lined up and ready to march.

"Come here!" an old party friend called to me.

I walked over to him.

"Aren't you marching today?" he asked me.

"I missed my union local," I told him.

"What the hell," he said. "March with us."

"I don't know," I said, remembering my last visit to the headquarters of the party, and my status as an "enemy."

"This is May Day," he said. "Get into the ranks."

"You know the trouble I've had," I said.

"That's nothing," he said. "Everybody's marching today."

"I don't think I'd better," I said, shaking my head.

"Are you scared?" he asked. "This is *May Day*."

He caught my right arm and pulled me into line beside him. I stood talking to him, asking about his work, about common friends.

"Get out of our ranks!" a voice barked.

I turned. A white Communist, a leader of the district of the Communist party, Cy Perry, a slender, close-cropped fellow, stood glaring at me.

"I—It's May Day and I want to march," I said.

"Get out!" he shouted.

"I was invited here," I said.

I turned to the Negro Communist who had invited me into the ranks. I did not want public violence. I looked at my friend. He turned his eyes away. He was afraid. I did not know what to do.

"You asked me to march here," I said to him.

He did not answer.

"Tell him that you did invite me," I said, pulling his sleeve.

"I'm asking you for the last time to get out of our ranks!" Cy Perry shouted.

I did not move. I had intended to, but I was beset by so many impulses that I could not act. Another white Communist came to assist Perry. Perry caught hold of my collar and pulled at me. I resisted. They held me fast. I struggled to free myself.

"Turn me loose!" I said.

Hands lifted me bodily from the sidewalk; I felt myself being pitched headlong through the air. I saved myself from landing on my head by clutching a curbstone with my hands. Slowly I rose and stood. Perry and his assistant were glaring at me. The rows of white and black Communists were looking at me with cold eyes of nonrecognition. I could not quite believe what had happened, even though my hands were smarting and bleeding. I had suffered a public, physical assault by two white Communists with black Communists looking on. I could not move from the spot. I was empty of any idea about what to do. But I did not feel belligerent. I had outgrown my childhood.

Suddenly, the vast ranks of the Communist party began to move. Scarlet banners with the hammer and sickle emblem of world revolution were lifted, and they fluttered in the May breeze. Drums beat. Voices were chanting. The tramp of many feet shook the earth. A long line of set-faced men and women, white and black, flowed past me.

I followed the procession to the Loop and went into Grant Park Plaza and sat upon a bench. I was not thinking; I could not think. But an objectivity of vision was being born within me. A surging sweep of many odds and ends came together and formed an attitude, a perspective. "They're blind," I said to myself. "Their enemies have blinded them with too much oppression." I lit a cigarette and I heard a song floating over the sunlit air:

Arise, you pris'ners of starvation!

I remembered the stories I had written, the stories in which I had assigned a role of honor and glory to the Communist party, and I was glad that they were down in black and white, were finished. For I knew in my heart that I should never be able to write that way again, should never be able to feel with that simple sharpness about life, should never again express such passionate hope, should never again make so total a commitment of faith.

A better world's in birth. . . .

The procession still passed. Banners still floated. Voices of hope still chanted.

I headed toward home alone, really alone now, telling myself that in all the sprawling immensity of our mighty continent the least-known factor of living was the human heart, the least-sought goal of being was a way to live a human life. Perhaps, I thought, out of my tortured feelings I could fling a spark into this darkness. I would try, not because I wanted to, but because I felt that I had to if I were to live at all.

I would hurl words into this darkness and wait for an echo; and if an echo sounded, no matter how faintly, I would send other words to tell, to march, to fight, to create a sense of the hunger for life that gnaws in us all, to keep alive in our hearts a sense of the inexpressibly human.

Walter White

Closely associated with James Weldon Johnson and Roy Wilkins in the NAACP as its Executive secretary, Walter White (1893-1955) combined literary facility with racial protest. Born in Atlanta, he attended Atlanta University and later studied at City College, New York. He looked so obviously Caucasian that some assumed that he had merely adopted the Negro race. He could very easily have "passed" into the white population just as thousands of very light-skinned Negroes had done, but he chose to identify himself wholeheartedly with the black and devoted his life to lightening the burdensome color line.

Of his two novels, *The Fire in the Flint* (1924) was an unusually successful antilynching story, and his experiences also made possible a nonfiction study of the same subject, *Rope and Faggot: A Biography of Judge Lynch* (1929). Like Johnson and Wilkins, he was an indefatigable investigator into lynchings and race riots for the NAACP. He lobbied patiently during the 1920's and 1930's for a federal antilynching law which occasionally got as far as the House but usually foundered upon a Senate filibuster. His white skin made it easy for him to gather confessions from lynchers in southern towns and villages where they were ready to boast of the latest brutalities. He won a reputation for always being promptly on the spot of a racial outbreak, as after the assassination of Harry T. Moore, the Florida NAACP head, and his wife in 1951.

This vivid selection, "Harlem Boils Over," comes from his autobiography, *A Man Called White* by Walter White (Copyright 1948 by Walter White. Reprinted by permission of The Viking Press, Inc. pp. 233-241). It is the astonishing first-hand account of the totally unexpected Harlem Riot of 1943, which was actually not a race riot but rather, as the reader soon discovers, a spontaneous explosion of sheer human misery.

Harlem Boils Over

On Sunday night, August 1, 1943, I went to bed early, exhausted in mind and body by three speaking engagements that day. I told Gladys that I did not want to be disturbed under any circumstances, even if President Roosevelt or Cleopatra called. I had been asleep only a few minutes when one of the members of our staff, Lucille Black, telephoned. Gladys told her of my request not to be disturbed and asked her to call back the next morning.

"But does Mr. White know there is a riot going on in Harlem?" Lucille asked.

Five minutes later I was dressed and ready to leave the house when Mayor La Guardia phoned asking me to meet him as quickly as possible at the West 123rd Street police station. Roy Wilkins joined me in the lobby and we took a cab to 125th Street and Seventh Avenue, where the worst of the rioting was then centered. Neither of us thought of it at the time we left the house, but it was fortunate for me that Roy was in the same taxicab. As we rode down Seventh Avenue we could hear the smashing of plate glass windows and the roar of the crowd, as far north as 135th Street. We saw Negroes attempting to get at white people in automobiles who, unaware of the riot, had driven into the heart of it. Our cab got through safely because Roy's brown skin saved us from attack.

Mayor La Guardia and Police Commissioner Lewis Valentine were already at the police station when we reached it. With the energy and resourcefulness which made him so great a mayor of New York, La Guardia had ordered all available police officers into the Harlem area and had telephoned Governor's Island for military police to get all soldiers and sailors out of Harlem. But unfortunately Governor's Island was sending only white MP's, and the temper of the crowds had already reached such a peak of frenzy that I feared mobs would attack them. I suggested to the Mayor that he telephone Governor's Island again to send an equal number of colored MP's and to issue instructions that they be assigned to work in racially mixed pairs. This was done and there was no instance of any trouble. Negroes could not object as violently, even to the use of force, if one of the two MP's handling a recalcitrant Negro soldier happened also to be a Negro.

Like many riots, this one had been caused by a wholly false rumor: that a Negro soldier had been shot in the back and killed without cause by a white policeman. There is in Harlem a hotel whose reputation has been questionable back to the days when that section of New York City was inhabited by whites. Unaware of its reputation, the mother of a Negro soldier stationed in New Jersey had gone there on Saturday night to await the arrival of her son from camp early the next morning. The soldier had brought his fiancée to the hotel for breakfast with his mother, after which the three had gone to church, visited friends, spent several pleasant hours at a moving picture theater, and then returned to the hotel to pick up the mother's luggage for her return home.

That afternoon a group of men and women had rented a room in the hotel for a drinking party. One of the women became intoxicated and boisterous. As the soldier with his mother and fiancée entered the lobby, the drunken woman was arguing vociferously with a policeman who was stationed on the premises because the hotel had been raided previously. The policeman in line with his duty was attempting to quiet the obstreperous female who was becoming increasingly abusive, as she appealed to other guests to "protect me from this white man!"

Not thoroughly informed nor understanding what was going on, the soldier remonstrated with the policeman who curtly advised him to mind his own business. Both men became angry and the policeman brandished his blackjack. The soldier seized the blackjack and started to run, whereupon the policeman, an inexperienced rookie, drew his revolver and shot the serviceman in the shoulder.

Under normal conditions the episode would have caused no more commotion than the average altercation that occurs in a huge city like New York scores of times daily. But conditions were far from normal in Harlem that sweltering summer night. A steady stream of letters had poured into the mailboxes of relatives and friends from Camp Stewart, Georgia, written by men of the 369th Infantry and telling of gratuitous insults and beatings and humiliations suffered by men who had fought in the Pacific and had been returned home to train other fighters. Not only Harlem's newspapers but the daily press had been filled with countless stories of lynchings and mistreatment of Negro soldiers. Long Island airplane factories and other war industries were begging for men and women workers, but those with black skins were daily told contemptuously that they were not wanted. These conditions existed while Harlem radios pleaded around the clock for Americans to do their utmost to win the war.

This was the caldron of brooding misery and frustration into which the rumor of another black soldier "murdered without provocation" was dropped. Down from the fire escapes where men and women sought futilely for a breath of fresh air, and out of the old-law tenements where color prejudice and poverty had packed human beings like sardines, poured an angry stream of Negroes. Fresh in their memories were the riots of Detroit and Beaumont, Texas, and the gory tales of black men hunted like wild beasts and killed. Symbols of a cruel and oppressive white world were the shiny plate-glass windows of the stores along 125th Street whose patronage was almost entirely Negro but many of which had refused bluntly to give employment to Negroes however qualified. Whatever missile could be found went hurtling through the windows, and the sound of crashing glass was like strong drink to the mob.

A strange and to me highly significant phenomenon was the fact that at the beginning of the riot, that is, from around ten P.M. on Sunday night until the early hours of the next morning, there was little looting. It was only after the first rage had spent itself that the looters became active. Throughout that first night food and clothing lay in tempting profusion behind smashed windows accessible to hordes of men and women who all their lives had been forced to work long hours at miserable pay to earn enough for bare subsistence. But the crowds, inflamed by injustice, real and fancied, were beyond greed, and their berserk rage found expression only in lashing out at the symbols of the hostile world which hemmed them in.

When the MP's had arrived and were sent out in pairs to round up servicemen, and assignments had been given to the steady stream of police officers who poured into the 28th Precinct police station, La Guardia suggested that he and I go on a tour of the area. Police Commissioner Valentine wanted to assign a squad car to precede and one to follow the Mayor's car for protection. The impetuous Mayor refused to wait the two or three minutes it would have taken to arrange this. I attempted to induce La Guardia to sit between me and the driver of the one-seat police car to avoid possible injury to the Mayor in the more exposed position. I was concerned not only for his sake, but also because I knew and feared the terrible publicity all Negroes would receive if any harm befell a man so well-known and beloved. But the Mayor would have none of this arrangement.

"They know my face better than yours," he ordered me, "so you sit in the middle."

Along Fifth, Lenox, and Madison Avenues north of 125th Street wild-eyed men and women, whose poverty was pathetically obvious in their shabbiness, roamed the streets, screaming imprecations. I thought of the stories I had read of the French Revolution when the starved hordes had poured from the sewers and slums of Paris, shouting their hatred of oppression and oppressors. As we drove up Lenox Avenue we heard the crash of a brick against a store front and La Guardia ordered the policeman to drive us to the spot. Although it took us but a minute or two to reach the scene, a fire broke out inside the store before the car came to a stop. Heedless of his own safety, La Guardia jumped from the car and screamed at the crowd before the building. I doubt that in the excitement the Mayor was recognized, but such was the fury with which he lashed out at the marauders that his moral indignation shamed and quieted the crowd, which rapidly dispersed.

It was apparent to me that the situation was becoming increasingly dangerous and that one-man campaigns to restore sanity, even when conducted by as popular a figure as Mayor La Guardia, could not stop the madness which had seized the community. I suggested to the Mayor that he order to Harlem city-owned sound trucks and that we get well-known Negro citizens to ride the streets of the area to appeal to the people to stop rioting and go home, explaining that the rumor which touched off the disorder was false. La Guardia thought this a good idea and asked us to round up as many well-known citizens of Harlem as possible. Roy and I got on the telephone, to learn to our disappointment that many of those we wanted, such as Duke Ellington, Adam Powell, Joe Louis, and Cab Calloway, were out of the city. But we got the Reverend John H. Johnson, rector of St. Martin's Protestant Episcopal Church; Parole Commissioner Samuel Battle; and Ferdinand Smith, secretary of the National Maritime Union.

Smith and I rode one sound truck together. Up Eighth Avenue from 123rd to 155th Street we cruised where the crowds were densest and angriest. Over and over again, as the huge vehicle nosed its way through crowded streets, we repeated our plea: "The rumor is false that a Negro soldier was killed at the Braddock Hotel tonight. He is only slightly wounded and is in no danger. Go to your homes! Don't form mobs or break the law! Don't destroy in one night the reputation as good citizens you have taken a lifetime to build! Go home—now!"

During our first trip up Eighth Avenue our pleas were greeted with raucous shouts of disbelief, frequently couched in language as violent as the action of the window-smashers. I remember particularly one giant of a man who stood on the sidewalk, his clenched fists raised in frenzied anger, and from whose face all semblance of patience had been stripped, leaving bare the fears and bitternesses which his dark skin had brought upon him. His voice was as loud as his body was big and strong, and the imprecations he hurled at us almost drowned the lesser voices of the others. He was still there when we came back down Eighth Avenue half an hour later, his upthrust arms still betokened his rage, but I fancied his face was slightly calmer and his language had diminished from obscenity to colorful profanity. The third time I saw him he was silent and his arms hung limply at his sides as he listened again to our statement that no Negro soldier had been killed that afternoon in Harlem.

Sheer repetition seemed to have its effect; on the second half of the second round trip, the giant was shouting to the thinning crowds to go home.

I began to notice also the cessation or at least the diminishing of another sound which had puzzled me—a rat-tat-tat on the roof of the sound truck as we moved into dense groups on the streets. It was the sound of missiles thrown at us from rooftops and windows of the tenements which lined Eighth Avenue and made it a canyon of poverty and sordid misery.

Toward morning the looters who always take advantage of disorder began to appear, especially from the more poverty-stricken areas east of Lenox Avenue. I remember especially a toothless old woman in front of a grocery store who moved about the edge of a crowd which had just smashed a store window. In one hand she clutched two grimy pillow cases which apparently she had snatched from the bed in which she had been sleeping. With the other hand she held the arm of a fourteen- or fifteen-year-old boy, possibly a grandson. The minute an opening appeared in the crowd the old woman, with an agility surprising in one of her age and emaciated appearance, climbed through the broken glass into the store window to fill the pillow cases with canned goods and cereals which lay in scattered disorder. When the bags were filled she turned toward the street and looked toward the police car in which La Guardia and I were sitting. Exultation, vengeance, the supreme satisfaction of having secured food for a few days, lighted her face, and then I looked at the sleepy-eyed child by her side. I felt nausea that an abundant society like America's could so degrade and starve a human being, and I was equally sickened to contemplate the kind of man the boy would become under such conditions.

By daylight the fury of the mob had spent itself. Mayor La Guardia and I went on the air in a broadcast to tell a startled New York what had happened. Over and over again the Mayor emphasized that the disorder had not been a race riot and to point out that no white person had been attacked nor had any white mob attempted to form. Both of us stated that resentment at the mistreatment of Negro soldiers, overcrowding, exorbitant rents, insufficient recreational facilities for both children and adults, poverty, and job proscription had caused the outbreak and that nothing could prevent its repetition except correction of these evils. Both press and radio handled the riot in the same sober and realistic fashion. I was amazed and delighted at the frequency of comment, ranging from husky taxi drivers to city officials, who said that they wondered why such an explosion had not occurred sooner considering the conditions under which the Negroes of Harlem lived.

Toward morning scores of prisoners were brought into the 28th Precinct station. Doctor Johnson, Mayor La Guardia, Commissioner Valentine, and I stood behind the desk watching the faces of the prisoners as they were booked. I have lived in Harlem since 1918, but I had never seen such concentrated despair as I witnessed that morning. Their anger spent, the men, women, and children were pathetic specimens of humanity as the consequences of their acts loomed before them. The loot which had been captured with them steadily mounted in the large lobby of the police station—clothing and household furnishings and food—particularly food. The majority of the citizens of Harlem awoke that morning stupefied at what had happened the night before because most of them had been at home in bed before the outbreak, totally unaware of the rioting.

The streets of Harlem where the rioting had been fiercest were a distressing sight in the glare of daylight. Ministers, social workers, newspapermen, housewives, and others, sickened with the disgrace which had been brought upon New York City and Negro citizens, begged to be assigned tasks to repair as far as possible the damage that had been done. We were faced with the immediate problem of getting food and particularly milk for children into the area where only a few of the stores were undamaged or unlooted. Some merchants whose property had escaped damage were fearful of opening their stores. It was significant that in the majority of cases those who had not been molested were the establishments which had not attempted to sell inferior goods at exorbitant prices and whose employment policies had been more liberal.

Under Mayor La Guardia's chairmanship a hastily arranged committee, through the New York City Department of Markets, made provisions for stocking the stores in Harlem with immediate necessities. It was not until late afternoon that we dared leave the scene to go to our homes to get baths and hot food and rest. Again on Monday night we patroled the streets which were then as quiet and empty as the financial district of lower Broadway on a Sunday morning.

As is usually the case, there were many meetings and conferences after the riot was over to discuss its causes and cures. The City-Wide Citizens Committee on Harlem was formed; it functioned for several years and did achieve some results in obtaining jobs for Negroes and in keeping before the consciousness of the people of New York the issues involved.

Algernon Black, leader of the Ethical Culture Society, and I were cochairmen for a while until the pressure of other work made it necessary for me to relinquish the responsibility. When I had to resign Dr. Black expressed his regret, saying, "The Black-White Committee is an ideal combination, especially since the man named 'Black' is white and the man named 'White' is black—or calls himself black."

But despite the efforts of individuals and organizations there has been little change in the basic causes of the 1943 riot in the thousands of Harlems—North and South—in the United States. Thrift of Negroes has been penalized by the attitude of banks, insurance companies, and investment corporations with respect to mortgages and other loans for improvement of housing in Harlem or other segregated areas in New York City. Restrictive covenants in deeds to property and the pressures of landlords and real estate agents continue to make it difficult if not impossible for Negroes, whatever their financial or cultural status, to purchase or rent property outside the ghetto. Amazingly and dishearteningly true is the fact that such covenants against Negroes have been used by members of other minorities who are themselves often the target of restrictive covenants.

More progress of a permanent nature has been made in the field of employment, but it is still a far higher hurdle for trained Negroes to utilize their training than for other Americans to do so. Yet I can see considerable progress when I look back at the situation in 1918 when I first arrived in New York. Today there are many more Americans who are aware that they too have a stake in the finding of a solution to the problem of the treatment of minorities in the United States and the world at large.

Ralph Johnson Bunche

Ralph Bunche (1904-—), Nobel Peace Prize winner and Under-Secretary of the United Nations, has been notably successful in attaining international distinction. A grandson of an American slave (with some Indian blood), he was born in Detroit on August 7, 1904; his father was a barber and his mother a musician. The family moved to Albuquerque, New Mexico, and after the death of both parents in 1916 he was raised as a self-reliant child by a strong-willed grandmother in Los Angeles. He worked his way through UCLA, specialized in international relations, especially in imperialism, starred in basketball, football, and other sports, won the Phi Beta Kappa award, and graduated *summa cum laude* in 1927. He later earned an M.A. and a Ph.D. in government at Harvard.

Academic grants enabled him to study native African tribes and other colonial peoples. From 1938 to 1940, he was chief staff member of the Carnegie Corporation of New York and chief aid to Dr. Gunnar Myrdal, the noted Swedish sociologist, in his monumental study of the American Negro. Meanwhile in 1937 he had become a political science professor at Howard University.

During World War II, Dr. Bunche served as an expert on African questions in the Office of Strategic Services. He attended the San Francisco Conference of 1945 on the UN as an expert on trusteeship questions and continued to serve the UN after its founding. Most important were his efforts as secretary of the UN Special Committee on Palestine in 1947. When Count Folke Bernadotte, the Palestinian Mediator, was killed on September 17, 1948, Bunche became acting Mediator and skillfully promoted a cease-fire order and a *de facto* peace between Arabs and Jews.

This selection is from his address of July 6, 1962, before the Atlanta Convention of the NAACP. It is reproduced by permission of Dr. Ralph J. Bunche. Here is a forthright statement by an outstanding Negro statesman of what the Negro of the Sixties wants.

NAACP Convention Address

I need scarcely mention the painfully obvious fact that school integration proceeds far too slowly. What has happened thus far in most places is only a token and a small token at that. Instead of all deliberate speed there has been a disgracefully deliberate dragging of feet. But this is a foolish tactic, for school integration in Georgia and Alabama and Mississippi and everywhere else is bound to come. Who then is losing from this procrastination against the law? Negro children, of course. But the community and nation even more, in the blow to morality and in the inevitable corrosion of respect for law which follows from organized contempt for it even by public officials sworn to uphold it.

Impatience, I do not doubt, has been a prime motivation in the heroic actions of Negro youth—and some white youth too—in the sit-down, bus boycott, freedom ride, campus strikes and demonstrations, and other protest activities of recent years—activities in which I have rejoiced because they marked a new awakening for the Negro and a courage in support of bold action; because they demonstrated conclusively that the Negro could no longer be intimidated and could, and readily would, laugh at and ridicule the Klansmen and their silly trappings and the futile threats of the white citizen councils alike.

Such demonstrations were not only timely, they were long overdue. Actions of this kind have accelerated the pace of progress in the achievement of social justice by dramatizing the struggle for the nation and all the world to see; they afford a convincing demonstration of the determination of the Negro to carry on the struggle for equality with ever more insistence, and the Negro's—and particularly the young Negro's—readiness to make costly sacrifices in that struggle.

I feel rather strongly that not enough has been done to honor those young people who, with such spontaneity and courage, rose to man the breastworks, so to speak, and to encourage youth to enroll in the continuing struggle in ever greater numbers. These many and largely anonymous young men and women are heroes, as genuine as any on battlefields. Their deeds must be kept fresh in our minds.

It is axiomatic in the process of social progress that the more the progress the more people will demand that it be quickened. This is a classical pattern in the development of the peoples of colonies toward emergence into independence and nationhood. It is equally true with regard to a minority ethnic group such as the American Negro. How long could anyone expect American Negro youth to be studying in schools and colleges about the glorious fruits of American democracy and be content with only the peelings? How long could it be expected that Negro youth would tolerate the absurd situations wherein their presence and money were sought after at sales counters in stores but they were unwelcome and their money refused at lunch counters and restaurants in those same stores? How could it be supposed that Negro youth would long stand for the indignity of the back seat in public transportation?

How could anyone in his senses expect young Negroes of this day and age, many of whom are called upon to give a couple of the best years of their lives to Uncle Sam's military service, to have their dignity as human beings assaulted at every turn and not defend it?

When I was age fourteen, my sister and I lost our parents and we were thereafter reared by our maternal grandmother. She was a tiny little woman physically, but a giant spiritually. She taught me many things, but the most important, I am sure, was the admonition to defend one's dignity at all costs. If you let anyone deprive you of your dignity, she would tell us, you lose your self-respect and there is then no moral strength left in you and you are less than a man. That counsel I will never forget and never ignore.

This, of course, is what the Negro is demanding—the complete right to human dignity, to self-respect, to be a man in full. We all know that this is possible only in a society in which there is entire equality, and this there must and will be. . . .

I have no mandate to speak on behalf of anyone but myself. But

I know what I, who have been for fifty-seven years an American of Negro ancestry, want and how I feel. I do not doubt that my wants and feelings are fairly representative of those of most of my race. I want to be a man on the same basis and level as any white citizen—I want to be as free as the whitest citizen. I want to exercise, and in full, the same rights as the white American. I want to be eligible for employment exclusively on the basis of my skills and employability, and for housing solely on my capacity to pay. I want to have the same privileges, the same treatment in public places as every other person. But this should not be read by anyone to mean that I want to be white; or that I am "pushy," seeking to go where I am not wanted. Far from it. I am as proud of my origin, ancestors, and race as anyone could be. Indeed, I resent nothing more than a racial slur or stigma. I want to go and to do only where and what all Americans are entitled to go and to do.

This I think is what every American Negro feels. It may be expressed in polite eloquence by some; in bitterness or even outright belligerence by others; it may cause some just to break out and start to knock things around. But in each case the emotion is sound and urgent and American.

I believe I could readily understand and accept this if I were not a Negro; if I were white. I can never really understand why the white man, whether from South or North, seems to find it difficult to do so. I am not sure that he does: it is possible that deep down in his heart he knows that the Negro cause is right and just. That, I think, may explain why there is so much less of racial tension in southern and northern communities today than there was a quarter century ago, despite the fact that the Negro is bolder and more demanding and that the walls of segregation have been often breached; why race riots do not occur; why Ku Klux Klansmen now just meekly hand out leaflets. I cannot understand how anyone claiming to be a good American can condone the denial of these elementals of democracy to any other American. How can anyone be so manifestly against the very essence of Americanism—not to mention fairness and decency—and at the same time purport to be fighting communism while thus giving to the Communists the strongest weapon they have against us? Negro citizens may be pardoned for expecting their white fellow citizens to be at least consistent.

The logic and the evidence are all against the race-baiting bitter-enders. It is so obvious that no one can miss it that the South, as it has reluctantly lowered some of its racial bars, is better off—politically, economically, and culturally—than it has ever been. The greatest resource of any community, state, or nation is its people, and it is recklessly shortsighted to waste that resource, as the South, and to only lesser extent the North, has been doing for so long. Depriving the Negro worker of fair employment costs the nation dearly in lost man-hours, production, consumption, and taxes.

I suppose I speak with an unavoidable bias, but I feel that if I were a white citizen in the South today, I would look at my black or brown brother and say to myself: what responsibility do I share for the crime that has been perpetrated not alone against this individual, but against the community and the nation? What have I contributed to the humiliation and degradation of this fellow American who except for a sheer accident of birth could be me or my brother? What can I do to rectify an injustice to the individual and a loss to the nation?

This being youth night, I really should close on a word especially for youth, although I do not care very much for distinctions among people, even on the basis of age. White or black, old or young, the real test comes in what you have done or can do. In a competitive world you must rise to meet the competition. That means preparation. It also means building up confidence on the basis of demonstrated performance. In connection with preparation, the school drop-out figures for Negro youth are alarming.

It is an exciting and inspiring world to be in. And, although there are great dangers in it, much tension and cause for worry, it affords vast opportunity—greater, I think, for youth, black as well as white, than has ever been known.

Ralph Ellison

Widely praised as one of the most gifted Negro novelists of our time, Ralph (Waldo) Ellison (1914-—) continues to win applause for his imaginative first novel *Invisible Man* (1952), with its subtle characterization of racial prejudice. He was born in Oklahoma City on March 1, 1914, studied at Tuskegee Institute, and then combined a literary career with frequent lecturing. He liked to speak on American Negro culture, particularly on Negro folklore. Universities have called upon him frequently to help direct their creative writing programs—he has done so at New York University, Columbia, Fisk, Antioch, Princeton, Bennington, and many others. In 1945 he held the Rosenwald Fellowship and in 1952 received the National Book Award for *Invisible Man*.

No other writer has expressed so imaginatively the dilemma of segregation, the isolation of the Negro, who is an invisible man in the white man's world. Here is a unique literary expression of social protest by a highly sensitive person.

Prologue to *Invisible Man*

I am an invisible man. No, I am not a spook like those who haunted Edgar Allan Poe; nor am I one of your Hollywood-movie ectoplasms. I am a man of substance, of flesh and bone, fiber and liquids—and I might even be said to possess a mind. I am invisible, understand, simply because people refuse to see me. Like the bodiless heads you see sometimes in circus sideshows, it is as though I have been surrounded by mirrors of hard, distorting glass. When they approach me they see only my surroundings, themselves, or figments of their imagination—indeed, everything and anything except me.

Nor is my invisibility exactly a matter of a biochemical accident to my epidermis. That invisibility to which I refer occurs because of a peculiar disposition of the eyes of those with whom I come in contact. A matter of the construction of their *inner* eyes, those eyes with which they look through their physical eyes upon reality. I am not complaining, nor am I protesting either. It is sometimes advantageous to be unseen, although it is most often rather wearing on the nerves. Then too, you're constantly being bumped against by those of poor vision. Or again, you often doubt if you really exist. You wonder whether you aren't simply a phantom in other people's minds. Say, a figure in a nightmare which the sleeper tries with all his strength to destroy. It's when you feel like this that, out of resentment, you begin to bump people back. And, let me confess, you feel that way most of the time. You ache with the need to convince yourself that you do exist in the real world, that you're a part of all the sound and anguish, and you strike out with your fists, you curse and you swear to make them recognize you. And, alas, it's seldom successful.

One night I accidentally bumped into a man, and perhaps because of the near darkness he saw me and called me an insulting name. I sprang at him, seized his coat lapels, and demanded that he apologize. He was a tall blond man, and as my face came close to his he looked insolently out of his blue eyes and cursed me, his breath hot in my face as he struggled. I pulled his chin down sharp upon the crown of my head, butting him as I had seen the West Indians do, and I felt his flesh tear and the blood gush out, and I yelled, "Apologize! Apologize!" But he continued to curse and struggle, and I butted him again and again until he went down heavily, on his knees, profusely bleeding. I kicked him repeatedly, in a frenzy because he still uttered insults though his lips were frothy with blood. Oh yes, I kicked him! And in my outrage I got out my knife and prepared to slit his throat, right there beneath the lamplight in the deserted street, holding him in the collar with one hand,

and opening the knife with my teeth—when it occurred to me that the man had not *seen* me, actually; that he, as far as he knew, was in the midst of a walking nightmare! And I stopped the blade, slicing the air as I pushed him away, letting him fall back to the street. I stared at him hard as the lights of a car stabbed through the darkness. He lay there, moaning on the asphalt; a man almost killed by a phantom. It unnerved me. I was both disgusted and ashamed. I was like a drunken man myself, wavering about on weakened legs. Then I was amused: Something in this man's thick head had sprung out and beaten him within an inch of his life. I began to laugh at this crazy discovery. Would he have awakened at the point of death? Would Death himself have freed him for wakeful living? But I didn't linger. I ran away into the dark, laughing so hard I feared I might rupture myself. The next day I saw his picture in the *Daily News,* beneath a caption stating that he had been "mugged." Poor fool, poor blind fool, I thought with sincere compassion, mugged by an invisible man!

Most of the time (although I do not choose as I once did to deny the violence of my days by ignoring it) I am not so overtly violent. I remember that I am invisible and walk softly so as not to awaken the sleeping ones. Sometimes it is best not to awaken them; there are few things in the world as dangerous as sleepwalkers. I learned in time though that it is possible to carry on a fight against them without their realizing it. For instance, I have been carrying on a fight with Monopolated Light & Power for some time now. I use their service and pay them nothing at all, and they don't know it. Oh, they suspect that power is being drained off, but they don't know where. All they know is that according to the master meter back there in their power station a hell of a lot of free current is disappearing somewhere into the jungle of Harlem. The joke, of course, is that I don't live in Harlem but in a border area. Several years ago (before I discovered the advantages of being invisible) I went through the routine process of buying service and paying their outrageous rates. But no more. I gave up all that, along with my apartment, and my old way of life: That way based upon the fallacious assumption that I, like other men, was visible. Now, aware of my invisibility, I live rent-free in a building rented strictly to whites, in a section of the basement that was shut off and forgotten during the nineteenth century, which I discovered when I was trying to escape in the night from Ras the Destroyer. But that's getting too far ahead of the story, almost to the end, although the end is in the beginning and lies far ahead.

The point now is that I found a home—or a hole in the ground, as you will. Now don't jump to the conclusion that because I call my home a "hole" it is damp and cold like a grave; there are cold holes and warm holes. Mine is a warm hole. And remember, a bear retires to his hole for the winter and lives until spring; then he comes strolling out like the Easter chick breaking from its shell. I say all this to assure you that it is incorrect to assume that, because I'm invisible and live in a hole, I am dead. I am neither dead nor in a state of suspended animation. Call me Jack-the-Bear, for I am in a state of hibernation.

My hole is warm and full of light. Yes, *full* of light. I doubt if there is a brighter spot in all New York than this hole of mine, and I do not exclude Broadway. Or the Empire State Building on a photographer's dream night. But that is taking advantage of you. Those two spots are among the darkest of our whole civilization—pardon me, our whole *culture* (an important distinction, I've heard) —which might sound like a hoax, or a contradiction, but that (by contradiction, I mean) is how the world moves: Not like an arrow, but a boomerang. (Beware of those who speak of the *spiral* of history; they are preparing a boomerang. Keep a steel helmet handy.) I know; I have been boomeranged across my head so much that I now can see the darkness of lightness. And I love light. Perhaps you'll think it strange that an invisible man should need light, desire light, love light. But maybe it is exactly because I *am* invisible. Light confirms my reality, gives birth to my form. A beautiful girl once told me of a recurring nightmare in which she lay in the center of a large dark room and felt her face expand until it filled the whole room, becoming a formless mass while her eyes ran in bilious jelly up the chimney. And so it is with me. Without light I am not only invisible, but formless as well; and to be unaware of one's form is to live a death. I myself, after existing some twenty years, did not become alive until I discovered my invisibility.

That is why I fight my battle with Monopolated Light & Power. The deeper reason, I mean: It allows me to feel my vital aliveness.

I also fight them for taking so much of my money before I learned to protect myself. In my hole in the basement there are exactly 1,369 lights. I've wired the entire ceiling, every inch of it. And not with fluorescent bulbs, but with the older, more-expensive-to-operate kind, the filament type. An act of sabotage, you know. I've already begun to wire the wall. A junk man I know, a man of vision, has supplied me with wire and sockets. Nothing, storm or flood, must get in the way of our need for light and ever more and brighter light. The truth is the light and light is the truth. When I finish all four walls, then I'll start on the floor. Just how that will go, I don't know. Yet when you have lived invisible as long as I have you develop a certain ingenuity. I'll solve the problem. And maybe I'll invent a gadget to place my coffee pot on the fire while I lie in bed, and even invent a gadget to warm my bed—like the fellow I saw in one of the picture magazines who made himself a gadget to warm his shoes! Though invisible, I am in the great American tradition of tinkers. That makes me kin to Ford, Edison, and Franklin. Call me, since I have a theory and a concept, a "thinker-tinker." Yes, I'll warm my shoes; they need it, they're usually full of holes. I'll do that and more.

Now I have one radio-phonograph; I plan to have five. There is a certain acoustical deadness in my hole, and when I have music I want to *feel* its vibration, not only with my ear but with my whole body. I'd like to hear five recordings of Louis Armstrong playing and singing "What Did I Do to Be So Black and Blue"—all at the same time. Sometimes now I listen to Louis while I have my favorite dessert of vanilla ice cream and sloe gin. I pour the red liquid over the white mound, watching it glisten and the vapor rising as Louis bends that military instrument into a beam of lyrical sound. Perhaps I like Louis Armstrong because he's made poetry out of being invisible. I think it must be because he's unaware that he *is* invisible. And my own grasp of invisibility aids me to understand his music.

Martin Luther King, Jr.

Back in the 1920's the Negro philosopher Alain Locke, of Howard University, wrote about the New Negro of the Harlem Renaissance, the determined man who had dropped traditional servility for the forthrightness of self-respect. By the 1960's no one seemed so representative of the New Negro as the Reverend Martin Luther King, Jr. (1929-—), of Montgomery, Alabama, whose bus boycott ignited the Negro Revolution. He was born in Atlanta, Georgia, the son of an independent-minded Baptist preacher and a schoolteacher mother. After graduating from Atlanta's Morehouse College, he decided upon a ministerial career, took graduate studies in liberal arts at Boston College and Harvard, and was ordained in 1947.

His congregation believed in their pastor's social emphasis upon race and community issues and joined the NAACP as a group. But despite the provocations of local racists, the Reverend King kept the tone of his sermons moderate, ever stressing the positive nonresistance of apostolic Christianity combined with the passive resistance of Mahatma Gandhi. The great opportunity to test Gandhian techniques came with the Montgomery bus strike of 1955, when King found a made-to-order situation of long-perpetuated humiliations shown Negro passengers. Success followed the boycott. His followers of the Southern Christian Leadership Conference chose Birmingham, the South's largest industrial center, for their great antisegregation drive of 1963. This followed Negro church bombings in Georgia, Florida, and other states. "If Birmingham could be cracked," King wrote, "the direction of the entire nonviolent movement in the South could take a significant turn." The Negro boycott crippled business and compelled merchants to negotiate a desegregation agreement for Negro jobs and the use of city recreational facilities, and to eliminate other Jim Crow practices. At the same time Attorney General Robert Kennedy pressed for the immediate registry of more than 2,000 Birmingham Negroes hitherto denied voting rights. Federal courts upheld the nonviolent demonstrations of Negroes here and elsewhere. Martin Luther King moved on to national leadership, undeterred by the bombings of his home. He organized committees to educate Negroes to register and vote; along economic lines he urged cooperative credit unions to enable Negroes to buy homes and businesses.

The great March on Washington of August 28, 1963, was intended to publicize the Negro's demand for an end to discrimination and segregation. The Reverend King, as president of the effective Southern Christian Leadership Conference, was a major sponsor of this movement, joining with the NAACP, the increasingly militant Urban League (up to recently conservative), the Congress of Racial Equality (CORE), and others in calling together peaceful crowds estimated at 200,000 to demonstrate. Other cities like Detroit too had their impressive Freedom Walk. In that heavily Negro city, about 125,000 rallied on June 23 to hear Martin Luther King speak in his simple direct way in behalf of a huge fund-raising campaign for civil rights.

This selection, "The Decisive Arrest," is the dramatic story of the Montgomery bus boycott of 1955 as told in King's book, *Stride Toward Freedom* (New York: Harper & Row, Publishers, Inc., 1958), pp. 43-46, 48-54. Copyright © 1958 by Martin Luther King, Jr. Reprinted by permission of Harper & Row, Publishers, Inc. The author tells of his historic decision to head the movement in behalf of Mrs. Rosa Parks—the beginning of the Negro Revolution of the Sixties.

The Decisive Arrest

On December 1, 1955, an attractive Negro seamstress, Mrs. Rosa Parks, boarded the Cleveland Avenue Bus in downtown Montgomery. She was returning home after her regular day's work in the Montgomery Fair—a leading department store. Tired from long hours on her feet, Mrs. Parks sat down in the first seat behind the section reserved for whites. Not long after she took her seat, the bus operator ordered her, along with three other Negro passengers, to move back in order to accommodate boarding white passengers. By this time every seat in the bus was taken. This meant that if Mrs. Parks followed the driver's command she would have to stand while a white male passenger, who had just boarded the bus, would sit. The other three Negro passengers immediately complied with the driver's request. But Mrs. Parks quietly refused. The result was her arrest.

There was to be much speculation about why Mrs. Parks did not obey the driver. Many people in the white community argued that she had been "planted" by the NAACP in order to lay the groundwork for a test case, and at first glance that explanation seemed plausible, since she was a former secretary of the local branch of the NAACP. So persistent and persuasive was this argument that it convinced many reporters from all over the country. Later on, when I was having press conferences three times a week—in order to accommodate the reporters and journalists who came to Montgomery from all over the world—the invariable first question was: "Did the NAACP start the bus boycott?"

But the accusation was totally unwarranted, as the testimony of both Mrs. Parks and the officials of the NAACP revealed. Actually, no one can understand the action of Mrs. Parks unless he realizes that eventually the cup of endurance runs over, and the human personality cries out, "I can take it no longer." Mrs. Parks's refusal to move back was her intrepid affirmation that she had had enough. It was an individual expression of a timeless longing for human dignity and freedom. She was not "planted" there by the NAACP, or any other organization; she was planted there by her personal sense of dignity and self-respect. She was anchored to that seat by the accumulated indignities of days gone by and the boundless aspirations of generations yet unborn. She was a victim of both the forces of history and the forces of destiny. She had been tracked down by the *Zeitgeist*—the spirit of the time.

Fortunately, Mrs. Parks was ideal for the role assigned to her by history. She was a charming person with a radiant personality, soft-spoken and calm in all situations. Her character was impeccable and her dedication deep-rooted. All of these traits together made her one of the most respected people in the Negro community.

Only E. D. Nixon—the signer of Mrs. Parks's bond—and one or two other persons were aware of the arrest when it occurred early Thursday evening. Later in the evening the word got around to a few influential women of the community, mostly members of the Women's Political Council. After a series of telephone calls back and forth they agreed that the Negroes should boycott the buses. They immediately suggested the idea to Nixon, and he readily concurred. In his usual courageous manner he agreed to spearhead the idea.

Early Friday morning, December 2, Nixon called me. He was so caught up in what he was about to say that he forgot to greet me with the usual "hello" but plunged immediately into the story of what had happened to Mrs. Parks the night before. I listened, deeply shocked, as he described the humiliating incident. "We have taken this type of thing too long already," Nixon concluded, his voice trembling. "I feel that the time has come to boycott the buses. Only through a boycott can we make it clear to the white folks that we will not accept this type of treatment any longer."

I agreed at once that some protest was necessary, and that the boycott method would be an effective one.

Just before calling me Nixon had discussed the idea with Rev. Ralph Abernathy, the young minister of Montgomery's First Baptist Church who was to become one of the central figures in the protest, and one of my closest associates. Abernathy also felt a bus boycott was our best course of action. So for thirty or forty minutes the three of us telephoned back and forth concerning plans and strategy. Nixon suggested that we call a meeting of all the ministers and civic leaders the same evening in order to get their thinking on the proposal, and I offered my church as the meeting place. The three of us got busy immediately. With the sanction of Rev. H. H. Hubbard—president of the Baptist Ministerial Alliance—Abernathy and I began calling all of the Baptist ministers. Since most of the Methodist ministers were attending a denomination meeting in one of the local churches that afternoon, it was possible for Abernathy to get the announcement to all of them simultaneously. Nixon reached Mrs. A. W. West—the widow of a prominent dentist—and enlisted her assistance in getting word to the civic leaders.

By early afternoon the arrest of Mrs. Parks was becoming public knowledge. Word of it spread around the community like uncontrolled fire. Telephones began to ring in almost rhythmic succession. By two o'clock an enthusiastic group had mimeographed leaflets concerning the arrest and the proposed boycott, and by evening these had been widely circulated.

As the hour for the evening meeting arrived, I approached the doors of the church with some apprehension, wondering how many of the leaders would respond to our call. Fortunately, it was one of those pleasant winter nights of unseasonable warmth, and to our relief, almost everybody who had been invited was on hand. More than forty people, from every segment of Negro life, were crowded into the large church meeting room. I saw physicians, schoolteachers, lawyers, businessmen, postal workers, union leaders, and clergymen. Virtually every organization of the Negro community was represented.

The largest number there was from the Christian ministry. Having left so many civic meetings in the past sadly disappointed by the dearth of ministers participating, I was filled with joy when I entered the church and found so many of them there; for then I knew that something unusual was about to happen.

Had E. D. Nixon been present, he would probably have been automatically selected to preside, but he had had to leave town earlier in the afternoon for his regular run on the railroad. In his absence, we concluded that Rev. L. Roy Bennett—as president of the Interdenominational Ministerial Alliance—was the logical person to take the chair. He agreed and was seated, his tall, erect figure dominating the room.

The meeting opened around seven thirty with H. H. Hubbard leading a brief devotional period. Then Bennett moved into action, explaining the purpose of the gathering. With excited gestures he reported on Mrs. Parks's resistance and her arrest. He presented the proposal that the Negro citizens of Montgomery should boycott the buses on Monday in protest. "Now is the time to move," he concluded. "This is no time to talk; it is time to act." . . .

I went home for the first time since seven that morning, and found Coretta relaxing from a long day of telephone calls and general excitement. After we had brought each other up to date on the day's developments, I told her, somewhat hesitantly—not knowing what her reaction would be—that I had been elected president of the new association. I need not have worried. Naturally surprised, she still saw that since the responsibility had fallen on me, I had no alternative but to accept it. She did not need to be told that we would now have even less time together, and she seemed undisturbed at the possible danger to all of us in my new position. "You know," she said quietly, "that whatever you do, you have my backing."

Reassured, I went to my study and closed the door. The minutes were passing fast. It was now six-thirty, and I had to leave no later than six-fifty to get to the meeting. This meant that I had only twenty minutes to prepare the most decisive speech of my life. As I thought of the limited time before me and the possible implications of this speech, I became possessed by fear. Each week I needed at least fifteen hours to prepare my Sunday sermon. Now I was faced with the inescapable task of preparing, in almost no time at all, a speech that was expected to give a sense of direction to a people imbued with a new and still unplumbed passion for justice. I was also conscious that reporters and television men would be there with their pencils and sound cameras poised to record my words and send them across the nation.

I was now almost overcome, obsessed by a feeling of inadequacy. In this state of anxiety, I had already wasted five minutes of the original twenty. With nothing left but faith in a power whose matchless strength stands over against the frailties and inadequacies of human nature, I turned to God in prayer. My words were brief and simple, asking God to restore my balance and to be with me in a time when I needed His guidance more than ever.

With less than fifteen minutes left, I began preparing an outline. In the midst of this, however, I faced a new and sobering dilemma: How could I make a speech that would be militant enough to keep my people aroused to positive action and yet moderate enough to keep this fervor within controllable and Christian bounds? I knew that many of the Negro people were victims of bitterness that could easily rise to flood proportions. What could I say to keep them courageous and prepared for positive action and yet devoid of hate and resentment? Could the militant and the moderate be combined in a single speech?

I decided that I had to face the challenge head on, and attempt to combine two apparent irreconcilables. I would seek to arouse the group to action by insisting that their self-respect was at stake and that if they accepted such injustices without protesting, they would betray their own sense of dignity and the eternal edicts of God Himself. But I would balance this with a strong affirmation of the Christian doctrine of love. By the time I had sketched an outline of the speech in my mind, my time was up. Without stopping to eat supper (I had not eaten since morning) I said good-by to Coretta and drove to the Holt Street Church.

Within five blocks of the church I noticed a traffic jam. Cars were lined up as far as I could see on both sides of the street. It was a moment before it occurred to me that all of these cars were headed for the mass meeting. I had to park at least four blocks from the church, and as I started walking I noticed that hundreds of people were standing outside. In the dark night, police cars circled slowly around the area, surveying the orderly, patient, and good-humored crowd. The three or four thousand people who could not get into the church were to stand cheerfully throughout the evening listening to the proceedings on the loud-speakers that had been set up outside for their benefit. And when, near the end of the meeting, these speakers were silenced at the request of the white people in surrounding neighborhoods, the crowd would still remain quietly, content simply to be present.

It took fully fifteen minutes to push my way through to the pastor's study, where Dr. Wilson told me that the church had been packed since five o'clock. By now my doubts concerning the continued success of our venture were dispelled. The question of calling off the protest was now academic. The enthusiasm of these thousands of people swept everything along like an onrushing tidal wave.

It was some time before the remaining speakers could push their way to the rostrum through the tightly packed church. When the meeting began it was almost half an hour late. The opening hymn was the old familiar "Onward Christian Soldiers," and when that mammoth audience stood to sing, the voices outside swelling the chorus in the church, there was a mighty ring like the glad echo of heaven itself.

Rev. W. F. Alford, minister of the Beulah Baptist Church, led the congregation in prayer, followed by a reading of the Scripture by Rev. U. J. Fields, minister of the Bell Street Baptist Church. Then the chairman introduced me. As the audience applauded, I rose and stood before the pulpit. Television cameras began to shoot from all sides. The crowd grew quiet.

Without manuscript or notes, I told the story of what had happened to Mrs. Parks. Then I reviewed the long history of abuses and insults that Negro citizens had experienced on the city buses. "But there comes a time," I said, "that people get tired. We are here this evening to say to those who have mistreated us so long that we are tired—tired of being segregated and humiliated; tired of being kicked about by the brutal feet of oppression." The congregation met this statement with fervent applause. "We had no alternative but to protest," I continued. "For many years, we have shown amazing patience. We have sometimes given our white brothers the feeling that we liked the way we were being treated. But we come here tonight to be saved from that patience that makes us patient with anything less than freedom and justice." Again the audience interrupted with applause.

Briefly I justified our actions, both morally and legally. "One of the great glories of democracy is the right to protest for right." Comparing our methods with those of the White Citizens Councils and the Ku Klux Klan, I pointed out that while "these organizations are protesting for the perpetuation of injustice in the community, we are protesting for the birth of justice in the community. Their methods lead to violence and lawlessness. But in our protest there will be no cross burnings. No white person will be taken from his home by a hooded Negro mob and brutally murdered. There will be no threats and intimidation. We will be guided by the highest principles of law and order."

With this groundwork for militant action, I moved on to words of caution. I urged the people not to force anybody to refrain from riding the buses. "Our method will be that of persuasion, not coercion. We will only say to the people, 'Let your conscience be your guide.'" Emphasizing the Christian doctrine of love, "our actions must be guided by the deepest principles of our Christian faith. Love must be our regulating ideal. Once again we must hear the words of Jesus echoing across the centuries: 'Love your enemies, bless them that curse you, and pray for them that despitefully use you.' If we fail to do this our protest will end up as a meaningless drama on the stage of history, and its memory will be shrouded with the ugly garments of shame. In spite of the mistreatment that we have confronted we must not become bitter, and end up by hating our white brothers. As Booker T. Washington said, 'Let no man pull you so low as to make you hate him.' " Once more the audience responded enthusiastically.

Then came my closing statement. "If you will protest courageously, and yet with dignity and Christian love, when the history books are written in future generations, the historians will have to pause and say, 'There lived a great people—a black people—who injected new meaning and dignity into the veins of civilization.' This is our challenge and our overwhelming responsibility." As I took my seat the people rose to their feet and applauded. I was thankful to God that the message had gotten over and that the task of combining the militant and the moderate had been at least partially accomplished. The people had been as enthusiastic when I urged them to love as they were when I urged them to protest.

As I sat listening to the continued applause I realized that this speech had evoked more response than any speech or sermon I had ever delivered, and yet it was virtually unprepared. I came to see for the first time what the older preachers meant when they said, "Open your mouth and God will speak for you." While I would not let this experience tempt me to overlook the need for continued preparation, it would always remind me that God can transform man's weakness into his glorious opportunity.

When Mrs. Parks was introduced from the rostrum by E. N. French, the audience responded by giving her a standing ovation. She was their heroine. They saw in her courageous person the symbol of their hopes and aspirations.

Now the time had come for the all-important resolution. Ralph Abernathy read the words slowly and forcefully. The main substance of the resolution called upon the Negroes not to resume riding the buses until (1) courteous treatment by the bus operators was guaranteed; (2) passengers were seated on a first-come, first-served basis—Negroes seated from the back of the bus toward the front while whites seated from the front toward the back; (3) Negro bus operators were employed on predominantly Negro routes. At the words "All in favor of the motion stand," every person to a man stood up, and those who were already standing raised their hands. Cheers began to ring out from both inside and outside. The motion was carried unanimously. The people had expressed their determination not to ride the buses until conditions were changed.

At this point I had to leave the meeting and rush to the other side of town to speak at a YMCA banquet. As I drove away my heart was full. I had never seen such enthusiasm for freedom. And yet this enthusiasm was tempered by amazing self-discipline. The unity of purpose and *esprit de corps* of these people had been indescribably moving. No historian would ever be able fully to describe this meeting and no sociologist would ever be able to interpret it adequately. One had to be a part of the experience really to understand it.

At the Ben Moore Hotel, as the elevator slowly moved up to the roof garden where the banquet was being held, I said to myself, the victory is already won, no matter how long we struggle to attain the three points of the resolution. It is a victory infinitely larger than the bus situation. The real victory was in the mass meeting, where thousands of black people stood revealed with a new sense of dignity and destiny.

Many will inevitably raise the question, why did this event take place in Montgomery, Alabama, in 1955? Some have suggested that the Supreme Court decision on school desegregation, handed down less than two years before, had given new hope of eventual justice to Negroes everywhere, and fired them with the necessary spark of encouragement to rise against their oppression. But although this might help to explain why the protest occurred when it did, it cannot explain why it happened in Montgomery.

Certainly, there is a partial explanation in the long history of injustice on the buses of Montgomery. The bus protest did not spring into being full grown as Athena sprang from the head of Zeus; it was the culmination of a slowly developing process. Mrs. Parks's arrest was the precipitating factor rather than the cause of the protest. The cause lay deep in the record of similar injustices. Almost everybody could point to an unfortunate episode that he himself had experienced or seen.

But there comes a time when people get tired of being trampled by oppression. There comes a time when people get tired of being plunged into the abyss of exploitation and nagging injustice. The story of Montgomery is the story of 50,000 such Negroes who were willing to substitute tired feet for tired souls, and walk the streets of Montgomery until the walls of segregation were finally battered by the forces of justice.

But neither is this the whole explanation. Negroes in other communities confronted conditions equally as bad, and often worse. So we cannot explain the Montgomery story merely in terms of the abuses that Negroes suffered there. Moreover, it cannot be explained by a preëxistent unity among the leaders, since we have seen that the Montgomery Negro community prior to the protest was marked by divided leadership, indifference, and complacency. Nor can it be explained by the appearance upon the scene of new leadership. The Montgomery story would have taken place if the leaders of the protest had never been born.

So every rational explanation breaks down at some point. There is something about the protest that is suprarational; it cannot be explained without a divine dimension. Some may call it a principle of concretion, with Alfred N. Whitehead; or a process of integration, with Henry N. Wieman; or Being-itself, with Paul Tillich; or a personal God. Whatever the name, some extrahuman force labors to create a harmony out of the discords of the universe. There is a creative power that works to pull down mountains of evil and level hilltops of injustice. God still works through history His wonders to perform. It seems as though God had decided to use Montgomery as the proving ground for the struggle and triumph of freedom and justice in America. And what better place for it than the leading symbol of the Old South? It is one of the splendid ironies of our day that Montgomery, the Cradle of the Confederacy, is being transformed into Montgomery, the cradle of freedom and justice.

The day of days, Monday, December 5, 1955, was drawing to a close. We all prepared to go to our homes, not yet fully aware of what had happened. The deliberations of that brisk, cool night in December will not be forgotten. That night we were starting a movement that would gain national recognition; whose echoes would ring in the ears of people of every nation; a movement that would astound the oppressor, and bring new hope to the oppressed. The night was Montgomery's moment in history.

A. Philip Randolph

There is no question that the vigorous, eloquent A. Philip Randolph (1889-—) is a genuine Negro leader with a large mass following, rather than an intellectual who depends upon the indirect influence of the written word. He was born in Crescent City, Florida, and moved to New York City, where he was educated at the College of the City of New York. Despite his opposition to segregation, he became in effect the head of the most segregated national union in 1925 when he organized the Brotherhood of Sleeping Car Porters as an essential step toward improved conditions and security for his race. His economic program became almost impossible with the rapid advance of railroad mechanization and the decline of passenger traffic.

His prestige rose in union ranks, especially after he had publicized his refusal to cooperate with Communist-infiltrated elements within the CIO; by 1957 he rose higher than any Negro had ever done in the labor movement when he became a vice president of the AFL-CIO organization. He even became a spokesman abroad for American labor of both races in 1951 when he presented the views of the American delegates to a world congress of the International Confederation of Free Trade Unions.

Throughout his life Randolph has been active in such race planning agencies as Mayor La Guardia's Commission on Race (1935). Perhaps most significant in his career to date was his militant direction of a proposed march on Washington which was averted when President Roosevelt initiated the Committee on Fair Employment Practices. This story is told, together with its aftermath, in his essay, "Why Should We March?" published in *Survey Graphic,* Vol. 31 (November 1942), 488-489, and reproduced here with the permission of A. Philip Randolph. The reader will note that certain of his desegregation objectives affecting the armed forces have already been realized, although other ideas, such as the stress on Negro representation in certain agencies, have not been recently prominent.

Why Should We March?

Though I have found no Negroes who want to see the United Nations[1] lose this war, I have found many who, before the war ends, want to see the stuffing knocked out of white supremacy and of empire over subject peoples. American Negroes, involved as we are in the general issues of the conflict, are confronted not with a choice but with the challenge both to win democracy for ourselves at home and to help win the war for democracy the world over.

There is no escape from the horns of this dilemma. There ought not to be escape. For if the war for democracy is not won abroad, the fight for democracy cannot be won at home. If this war cannot be won for the white peoples, it will not be won for the darker races.

Conversely, if freedom and equality are not vouchsafed the peoples of color, the war for democracy will not be won. Unless this double-barreled thesis is accepted and applied, the darker races will never wholeheartedly fight for the victory of the United Nations. That is why those familiar with the thinking of the American Negro have sensed his lack of enthusiasm, whether among the educated or uneducated, rich or poor, professional or nonprofessional, religious or secular, rural or urban, north, south, east or west.

That is why questions are being raised by Negroes in church, labor union, and fraternal society; in poolroom, barbershop, schoolroom, hospital, hair-dressing parlor; on college campus, railroad, and bus. One can hear such questions asked as these: What have Negroes to fight for? What's the difference between Hitler and that "cracker" Talmadge of Georgia? Why has a man got to be Jim-Crowed to die for democracy? If you haven't got democracy yourself, how can you carry it to somebody else?

What are the reasons for this state of mind? The answer is: dis-

[1] The Allies.

crimination, segregation, Jim Crow. Witness the navy, the army, the air corps; and also government services at Washington. In many parts of the South, Negroes in Uncle Sam's uniform are being put upon, mobbed, sometimes even shot down by civilian and military police, and on occasion lynched. Vested political interests in race prejudice are so deeply entrenched that to them winning the war against Hitler is secondary to preventing Negroes from winning democracy for themselves. This is worth many divisions to Hitler and Hirohito. While labor, business, and farm are subjected to ceilings and doors and not allowed to carry on as usual, these interests trade in the dangerous business of race hate as usual.

When the defense program began and billions of the taxpayers' money were appropriated for guns, ships, tanks, and bombs, Negroes presented themselves for work only to be given the cold shoulder, North as well as South; and despite their qualifications, Negroes were denied skilled employment. Not until their wrath and indignation took the form of a proposed protest march on Washington, scheduled for July 1, 1941, did things begin to move in the form of defense jobs for Negroes. The march was postponed by the timely issuance (June 25, 1941) of the famous Executive Order No. 8802 by President Roosevelt. But this order and the President's Committee on Fair Employment Practice, established thereunder, have as yet only scratched the surface by way of eliminating discriminations on account of race or color in war industry. Both management and labor unions in too many places and in too many ways are still drawing the color line.

It is to meet this situation squarely with direct action that the March on Washington Movement launched its present program of protest mass meetings. Twenty thousand were in attendance at Madison Square Garden, June 16; sixteen thousand in the Coliseum in Chicago, June 26; nine thousand in the City Auditorium of St. Louis, August 14. Meetings of such magnitude were unprecedented among Negroes.[2] The vast throngs were drawn from all walks and levels of Negro life—businessmen, teachers, laundry workers, Pull-

[2] In view of charges made that they were subsidized by Nazi funds, it may not be amiss to point out that of the $8,000 expenses of the Madison Square meeting every dime was contributed by Negroes themselves, except for tickets bought by some liberal white organizations.

man porters, waiters, and red caps; preachers, crapshooters, and social workers; jitterbugs and Ph.D's. They came and sat in silence, thinking, applauding only when they considered the truth was told, when they felt strongly that something was going to be done about it.

The March on Washington Movement is essentially a movement of the people. It is all Negro and pro-Negro, but not for that reason anti-white or anti-Semitic, or anti-Catholic, or anti-foreign, or anti-labor. Its major weapon is the nonviolent demonstration of Negro mass power. Negro leadership has united back of its drive for jobs and justice. "Whether Negroes should march on Washington, and if so, when?" will be the focus of a forthcoming national conference. For the plan of a protest march has not been abandoned. Its purpose would be to demonstrate that American Negroes are in deadly earnest, and all out for their full rights. No power on earth can cause them today to abandon their fight to wipe out every vestige of second class citizenship and the dual standards that plague them.

A community is democratic only when the humblest and weakest person can enjoy the highest civil, economic, and social rights that the biggest and most powerful possess. To trample on these rights of both Negroes and poor whites is such a commonplace in the South that it takes readily to anti-social, anti-labor, anti-Semitic, and anti-Catholic propaganda. It was because of laxness in enforcing the Weimar constitution in republican Germany that Nazism made headway. Oppression of the Negroes in the United States, like suppression of the Jews in Germany, may open the way for a fascist dictatorship.

By fighting for their rights now, American Negroes are helping to make America a moral and spiritual arsenal of democracy. Their fight against the poll tax, against lynch law, segregation, and Jim Crow, their fight for economic, political, and social equality, thus becomes part of the global war for freedom.

Program of the March on Washington Movement

1. We demand, in the interest of national unity, the abrogation of every law which makes a distinction in treatment between citizens based on religion, creed, color, or national origin. This means an end

to Jim Crow in education, in housing, in transportation, and in every other social, economic, and political privilege; and especially, we demand, in the capital of the nation, an end to all segregation in public places and in public institutions.

2. We demand legislation to enforce the Fifth and Fourteenth Amendments guaranteeing that no person shall be deprived of life, liberty, or property without due process of law, so that the full weight of the national government may be used for the protection of life and thereby may end the disgrace of lynching.

3. We demand the enforcement of the Fourteenth and Fifteenth Amendments and the enactment of the Pepper Poll Tax bill so that all barriers in the exercise of the suffrage are eliminated.

4. We demand the abolition of segregation and discrimination in the army, navy, marine corps, air corps, and all other branches of national defense.

5. We demand an end to discrimination in jobs and job training. Further, we demand that the FEPC be made a permanent administrative agency of the U. S. Government and that it be given power to enforce its decisions based on its findings.

6. We demand that federal funds be withheld from any agency which practices discrimination in the use of such funds.

7. We demand colored and minority group representation on all administrative agencies so that these groups may have recognition of their democratic right to participate in formulating policies.

8. We demand representation for the colored and minority racial groups on all missions, political and technical, which will be sent to the peace conference so that the interests of all people everywhere may be fully recognized and justly provided for in the post-war settlement.

James Baldwin

In the contemporary literature of the Negro's righteous anger, perhaps no novelist or essayist has eclipsed the poetic sensitivity and articulateness of James (Arthur) Baldwin (1924- —) of New York. He was born in New York City on August 2, 1924, and raised in the segregated squalor of Harlem (which has inspired a generation of young Negro writers). In elementary and high school he showed precocious talents for writing. Even his absorption in supporting a family did not prevent him from writing excellent articles, plays, stories, and sketches. Fortunately he was aided by generous literary fellowships.

As a young man he became well-known to readers of *Partisan Review, Harper's,* and the *American Mercury*. His first book, *Go Tell It on the Mountain* (Knopf, 1953) combined realism and poetic feeling in a story of religious experience in Harlem that was enthusiastically received. Two years later appeared *Notes of a Native Son* (Beacon Press, 1955), which was even more successful, receiving praise for its "bitter clarity and uncommon grace." This book contains acid sketches as well as gentle ones of the Harlem ghetto and a sensitive expression of the alienated northern Negro intellectual lacking roots in either America or Africa.

In recent years James Baldwin's pen has expressed the militancy of the younger generation. Some of his striking magazine articles on race philosophy and Negro strategy were collected in *Nobody Knows My Name* (New York: Dial Press, Inc., 1963); a selection from pages 86-89 and 98-99 of this book is presented here with the permission of Dial Press, Inc. and Michael Joseph Ltd. of London. Copyright © 1959, 1961 by James Baldwin. Especially noteworthy is the author's attempt to understand his southern ancestry.

Nobody Knows My Name:
A Letter From the South

I walked down the street, didn't have on no hat,
Asking everybody I meet,
Where's my man at?

—Ma Rainey

Negroes in the North are right when they refer to the South as the Old Country. A Negro born in the North who finds himself in the South is in a position similar to that of the son of the Italian emigrant who finds himself in Italy, near the village where his father first saw the light of day. Both are in countries they have never seen, but which they cannot fail to recognize. The landscape has always been familiar; the speech is archaic, but it rings a bell; and so do the ways of the people, though their ways are not his ways. Everywhere he turns, the revenant finds himself reflected. He sees himself as he was before he was born, perhaps or as the man he would have become, had he actually been born in this place. He sees the world, from an angle odd indeed, in which his fathers awaited his arrival, perhaps in the very house in which he narrowly avoided being born. He sees, in effect, his ancestors, who, in everything they do and are, proclaim his inescapable identity. And the northern Negro in the South sees, whatever he or anyone else may wish to believe, that his ancestors are both white and black. The white men, flesh of his flesh, hate him for that very reason. On the other hand, there is scarcely any way for him to join the black community in the South: for both he and this community are in the grip of the immense illusion that their state is more miserable than his own.

This illusion owes everything to the great American illusion that our state is a state to be envied by other people: we are powerful, and we are rich. But our power makes us uncomfortable and we handle it very ineptly. The principal effect of our material well-being has been to set the children's teeth on edge. If we ourselves were not so fond of this illusion, we might understand ourselves and other peoples better than we do, and be enabled to help them understand us. I am very often tempted to believe that this illusion is all that is left of the great dream that was to have become America; whether this is so or not, this illusion certainly prevents us from making America what we say we want it to be.

But let us put aside, for the moment, these subversive speculations. In the fall of last year, my plane hovered over the rust-red earth of Georgia. I was past thirty, and I had never seen this land before. I pressed my face against the window, watching the earth come closer; soon we were just above the tops of trees. I could not suppress the thought that this earth had acquired its color from the blood that had dripped down from these trees. My mind was filled with the image of a black man, younger than I, perhaps, or my own age, hanging from a tree, while white men watched him and cut his sex from him with a knife.

My father must have seen such sights—he was very old when he died—or heard of them, or had this danger touch him. The Negro poet I talked to in Washington, much younger than my father, perhaps twenty years older than myself, remembered such things very vividly, had a long tale to tell, and counseled me to think back on those days as a means of steadying the soul. I was to remember that time, whatever else it had failed to do, nevertheless had passed, that the situation, whether or not it was better, was certainly no longer the same. I was to remember that southern Negroes had endured things I could not imagine; but this did not really place me at such a great disadvantage, since they clearly had been unable to imagine what awaited them in Harlem. I remembered the Scottsboro case, which I had followed as a child. I remembered Angelo Herndon and wondered, again, whatever had become of him. I remembered the soldier in uniform blinded by an enraged white man, just after the Second World War. There had been many such incidents after the First War, which was one of the reasons I had been born in Harlem. I remembered Willie McGhee, Emmett Till, and the others. My younger brothers had visited Atlanta some years before. I remembered what they had told me about it. One of my brothers, in uniform, had had his front teeth kicked out by a white officer. I remembered my mother telling us how she had wept and prayed and tried to kiss the venom out of her suicidally embittered son. (She managed to do it, too; heaven only knows what she herself was feeling, whose father and brothers had lived and died down here.) I remembered myself as a very small boy, already so bitter about the pledge of allegiance that I could scarcely bring myself to say it, and never, never believed it.

I was, in short, but one generation removed from the South, which was now undergoing a new convulsion over whether black children had the same rights, or capacities, for education as did the children of white people. This is a criminally frivolous dispute, absolutely unworthy of this nation; and it is being carried on, in complete bad faith, by completely uneducated people. (We do not trust educated people and rarely, alas, produce them, for we do not trust the independence of mind which alone makes a genuine education possible.) Educated people, of any color, are so extremely rare that it is unquestionably one of the first tasks of a nation to open all of its schools to all of its citizens. But the dispute has actually nothing to do with education, as some among the eminently uneducated know. It has to do with political power and it has to do with sex. And this is a nation which, most unluckily, knows very little about either.

The city of Atlanta, according to my notes, is "big, wholly segregated, sprawling; population variously given as six hundred thousand or one million, depending on whether one goes beyond or remains within the city limits. Negroes 25 to 30 per cent of the population. Racial relations, on the record, can be described as fair, considering that this is the state of Georgia. Growing industrial town. Racial relations manipulated by the mayor and a fairly strong Negro middle class. This works mainly in the areas of compromise and concession and has very little effect on the bulk of the Negro population and none whatever on the rest of the state. No integration, pending or actual." Also, it seemed to me that the Negroes in Atlanta were "very vividly *city* Negroes"—they seemed less patient than their rural brethren, more dangerous, or at least more unpredictable. And: "Have seen one wealthy Negro section, very pretty, but with an unpaved road. . . . The section in which I am living is composed of frame houses in various stages of disrepair and neglect, in which two and three families live, often sharing a single toilet. This is the other side of the tracks; literally, I mean. It is located, as I am told is the case in many southern cities, just beyond the underpass." Atlanta contains a high proportion of Negroes who own their own homes and exist, visibly anyway, independently of the white world. Southern towns distrust this class and do everything in their power to prevent its appearance. But it is a class which has a certain usefulness in southern cities. There is an incipient war, in fact, between southern cities and southern towns—between the city, that is, and the state—which we will discuss later. Little Rock is an ominous example of this and it is likely—indeed, it is certain—that we will see many more such examples before the present crisis is over. . . .

Many of the parents listen to speeches by people like Senator Russell and find themselves unable to sleep at night. They are in the extraordinary position of being compelled to work for the destruction of all they have bought so dearly—their homes, their comfort, the safety of their children. But the safety of their children is merely comparative; it is all that their comparative strength as a class has bought them so far; and they are not safe, really, as long as the bulk of Atlanta's Negroes live in such darkness. On any night, in that other part of town, a policeman may beat up one Negro too many, or some Negro or some white man may simply go berserk. This is all it takes to drive so delicately balanced a city mad. And the island on which these Negroes have built their handsome houses will simply disappear.

This is not at all in the interests of Atlanta, and almost everyone there knows it. Left to itself, the city might grudgingly work out compromises designed to reduce the tension and raise the level of Negro life. But it is not left to itself; it belongs to the state of Georgia. The Negro vote has no power in the state, and the governor of Georgia—that "third-rate man," Atlantans call him—makes great political capital out of keeping the Negroes in their place. When six Negro ministers attempted to create a test case by ignoring the segregation ordinance on the buses, the governor was ready to declare martial law and hold the ministers incommunicado. It was the mayor who prevented this, who somehow squashed all publicity, treated the ministers with every outward sign of respect, and it is his office which is preventing the case from coming into court. And remember that it was the governor of Arkansas, in an insane bid for political power, who created the present crisis in Little Rock—against the will of most of its citizens and against the will of the mayor.

This war between the southern cities and states is of the utmost importance, not only for the South, but for the nation. The southern states are still very largely governed by people whose political lives, insofar, at least, as they are able to conceive of life or politics, are dependent on the people in the rural regions. It might, indeed, be more honorable to try to guide these people out of their pain and ignorance instead of locking them within it, and battening on it; but it is, admittedly, a difficult task to try to tell people the truth and it is clear that most southern politicians have no intention of attempting it. The attitude of these people can only have the effect of stiffening the already implacable Negro resistance, and this attitude is absolutely certain, sooner or later, to create great trouble in the cities. When a race riot occurs in Atlanta, it will not spread merely to Birmingham, for example. (Birmingham is a doomed city.) The trouble will spread to every metropolitan center in the nation which has a significant Negro population. And this is not only because the ties between northern and southern Negroes are still very close. It is because the nation, the entire nation, has spent a hundred years avoiding the question of the place of the black man in it.

That this has done terrible things to black men is not even a question. "Integration," said a very light Negro to me in Alabama, "has always worked very well in the South, after the sun goes down." "It's not miscegenation," said another Negro to me, "unless a black man's involved." Now, I talked to many southern liberals who were doing their best to bring integration about in the South, but met scarcely a single southerner who did not weep for the passing of the old order. They were perfectly sincere, too, and, within their limits, they were right. They pointed out how Negroes and whites in the South had loved each other, they recounted to me tales of devotion and heroism which the old order had produced, and which, now, would never come again. But the old black men I looked at down there—those same black men that the southern liberal had loved; for whom, until now, the southern liberal—and not only the liberal—has been willing to undergo great inconvenience and danger—they were not weeping. Men do not like to be protected, it emasculates them. This is what black men know, it is the reality they have lived with; it is what white men do not want to know. It is not a pretty thing to be a father and be ultimately dependent on the power and kindness of some other man for the well-being of your house.

But what this evasion of the Negro's humanity has done to the nation is not so well-known. The really striking thing, for me, in the South was this dreadful paradox, that the black men were stronger than the white. I do not know how they did it, but it certainly has something to do with that as yet unwritten history of the Negro woman. What it comes to, finally, is that the nation has spent a large part of its time and energy looking away from one of the principal facts of its life. This failure to look reality in the face diminishes a nation as it diminishes a person, and it can only be described as unmanly. And in exactly the same way that the South imagines that it "knows" the Negro, the North imagines that it has set him free. Both camps are deluded. Human freedom is a complex, difficult—and private—thing. If we can liken life, for a moment, to a furnace, then freedom is the fire which burns away illusion. Any honest examination of the national life proves how far we are from the standard of human freedom with which we began. The recovery of this standard demands of everyone who loves this country a hard look at himself, for the greatest achievements must begin somewhere, and they always begin with the person. If we are not capable of this examination, we may yet become one of the most distinguished and monumental failures in the history of nations.

Elijah Muhammed

The Black Muslim spokesman for the uprooted and frustrated urban Negro, Elijah Poole, known as Elijah Muhammed (1897- —), was born in rural Georgia the son of a Baptist minister. His formal education ended at the eighth grade, but perhaps his real education began in the Detroit Negro ghetto when one of the numerous Negro Moslem cultists, Fard Muhammed, "Allah in Person," took him under his wing in the first Temple of Islam built in that city. After Elijah moved to Chicago, he claimed to be Fard's successor as "Elijah Muhammed" and took up the cause of black nationalism, attacking the "white man's war" and urging Negroes not to serve. Yet this powerful and influential personality seemed to be a small, mild man who habitually spoke in a calm voice in private conversation. Together with his six able sons and an extraordinary lieutenant, Malcolm X, he succeeded in building the elaborate Black Muslim organization of "ministers" and other titled subordinates.

Elijah Muhammed's Chicago still contained thousands of followers of the deported Messiah, Marcus Garvey, who believed in the tenets of black supremacy and gladly joined the new Black Muslim movement. Not only did these racists find ideas and inspiration in the Ku Klux Klan and Nazi-style causes, but they even cooperated on occasion with Bilbo-inspired congressional proposals for a back-to-Africa movement of Negroes. The Black Muslims, like the Klan, presented themselves as the shield of female chastity, good domestic morals, and racial pride. If the white racists held that the Negro was at the bottom of the evolutionary scale, the followers of Elijah Muhammed argued that the African Negro was at the apex of evolution and that the white man belonged to the Devil. They repudiated American society, rejected Christianity as a hypocritical religion concerned only with a white God, denounced integrationists as Uncle Toms, charged that the NAACP was a tool of the Zionists (they even made sympathetic contact with Nasser), and encouraged anti-Semitism by picturing the Jew as an exploiter of cheap Negro labor.

More significant was the effort of the Black Muslims to raise the self-respect and well-being of inhabitants of the black ghetto—to correct the disorganization of broken homes, the apathy, youthful defiance and predatory habits, the widespread ill health, unemployment, chronic poverty, illiteracy, and the frustrations wrought by white discriminations. Elijah Muhammed aroused enthusiasm by his assurances of Negro superiority, the daily accounts recorded in his organ, *Muhammed Speaks,* of anti-Negro persecution, and his injunctions for self-rehabilitation as well as by his apocalyptic utterances. His parochial schools in Chicago, the "University of Islam," taught children Arabic beginning in the third grade and created an attractive image of the Negro past rooted in a rich Moslem culture, thus showing that the black was not "the-so-called Negro" at all. Muhammed's spoken or written messages and those of his ministers came frequently over the radio and television, and through newspapers and huge public lectures and demonstrations. Through successful cooperative ventures Elijah Muhammed followed the self-help philosophy of Booker T. Washington (Garvey, too, had once written that he was influenced by reading *Up From Slavery*), establishing Negro department stores and large apartment houses, and encouraging Negroes to become small capitalists. Black Muslims were taught to eschew alcohol, tobacco, drugs, swearing, gambling, dancing, cosmetics, extramarital relations, and eating the pork, cornbread, and greens familiar to the southern Negro, and to avoid hair-straightening, the mark of the integrationist. Like Booker T. Washington, he urged cleanliness, hard work, regular habits, sobriety, and virtuous family life. Thus the Black Muslims embraced the segregationism of the famous Tuskegee leader (who was under attack from integrationists), his capitalist ideas, and even his injunctions to avoid violence, although they rejected his theories of collaboration or accommodation with white leaders.

The selections below are from Elijah Muhammed's writings in *Muhammed Speaks*. They include his addresses of March 13 and March 28, 1964, which allude to a separate land for Negroes; strict separation of the races; the Negro's complete alienation from America; pacifism; the gross error of Martin Luther King, Jr., in appealing to Negroes to love their enemies; the inspiration of the new African states; and the harmfulness of the civil rights movements. The Black Muslim program is summarized clearly in "What the Muslims Want" and "What the Muslims Believe." These are published by permission of the editor of *Muhammed Speaks*. Readers must decide whether these ideas express a variant of Negro cultism of the Harlem variety, nationalism analogous to the contemporary African movements, fascism of the Nazi type, or possibly a unique racial philosophy.

I. Highlights of Elijah Muhammed's Address, March 28, 1964

* * *

I say to you who think that I am begging for some of these states, as I read in the papers—I am not begging for states. It is immaterial to me, if the white government of America does not want to give us anything, just let us go. We will make a way. Our God will make a way for us.

I am not going to start a war with them to take land, because all of it belongs to us. I say to the government that if they cannot agree on giving us justice and agree on giving us a chance to make a living for ourselves as they are for themselves, with freedom, justice, and equality—as they have, then let us go. Let us go back to our native land and people. Every Muslim can go. We, the Muslims, are the true owners of the heavens and the earth.

* * *

I give the white people credit. They do the best they can in some instances, but at the same time, I can't say that they are angels. They have jailed us, bound us up among them. They should take care of us, to give us a chance. If not, they should let us go.

* * *

Don't tell me that we are equal. We are not equal. We can't be equal. How can we be equal when they own everything and we own nothing?

We have enough educated black men and women in this government to start a government big enough to take care of the world.

* * *

War is due. War is inevitable. There can be no showdown here in America until your problem is solved. He (Allah) has made me a Door. If you get out, you will come by me; and if you reject me, you won't go. I have been given the keys to heaven.

* * *

This white government has ruled us and given us plenty hell, but the time has arrived that you taste a little of your own hell. The only way that America could have an extension of time. I guess you think I am acting. No, I am not acting like a judge, but I heard what the Judge said.

If America attacks any nation, she will herself be shot to pieces. For centuries she has boasted that she has made other nations bow at her feet. Now God wants to show the others that He will make you bow. It would be wise for you if you want to get an extension of time to treat us right. And if you want to hasten your time—shoot us. Shoot Elijah. Kill us all. Kill all of my followers and Elijah will go down laughing and knowing that this is the end of you.

* * *

All of my followers have been questioned by the FBI. Just what are you trying to do? You want to find out just how weak or how strong we are?

We want the FBI to know what we are teaching. We are not teaching what we do not want you to know, FBI. We want the government to know we have no secrets. The thing that you should do, you should try to keep it a secret yourself—when you can.

* * *

Do you think that I am happy knowing that you are behind me, trying to keep my followers from following me? I am not happy about you trying to take my followers—carrying them with you because I KNOW where you're going.

Now the white people want to marry Negroes. Negroes who have no knowledge of themselves want to marry white folks. It's like a frog wanting to marry a rattlesnake because the rattlesnake is so full of frogs 'til he can't swallow another one.

The whole world is angry. We must have a showdown. We have got to have it. We want to live in peace.

Every day of our lives we are at your mercy. An army of policemen throughout the country with a club in their hands set out to beat "nigger" heads, not to beat white folks' heads—"nigger" heads and to shoot the "nigger" if he feels like it.

Nothing hindering him. He's not going to go to prison for doing it. All he has to do is to tell the judge that he shot that old "nigger" and the judge will wink his eye at him and say "Wish I had of had a chance to shoot him myself." This is the kind of people we are living with. With murderers, not friends, but murderers.

Look at the southern Senators saying that they will sit down and stay there night and day before ever they agree to give the Negro civil rights.

There are many of my poor black ignorant brothers—and even preachers—preaching the ignorant and lying stuff that you should love your enemy. What fool can love his enemy?

Martin Luther calls himself a preacher and has written a book to try to fool you—to make you love the devil himself. How can Martin Luther, being the minister he claims of God, teach his people to love their enemy, when God Himself said he had set a day to deal with his enemies. And he said himself, according to the Bible that Martin Luther reads, that there were two brothers—I loved one and hated the other.

* * *

I want to know from you, why so much about hate teachings? It's hate teachings, you say. It's race teachings. I want to know, if you were born in America as I was—all your life you have been hated by white people—and you are hated by them today. Here comes the truth of the white man, making you to know that he cannot love you, that he is the devil himself.

Now, you say, no, no, he is not the devil—God said he was. They say we teach that he is the blue-eyed devil. I did not make him.

They say that I am teaching you all to hate the devil. But when did they ever love our people? I will most certainly not teach you to love the devil.

* * *

They are doing everything they possibly can—and I don't care if the entire white race hears me say this, they are doing everything they possibly can to deceive the poor old Negro.

We are happy, we the Muslims. We know we have a Savior.

This day, 87 years ago, a Savior was born . . . to go after that particular people that was lost and swallowed up by Israel, seeking something that did not belong to Israel . . . not seeking any but His own particular people. . . .

A Savior is born, not to save the Jews, but to save the poor Negro.

I am here to teach the way back to the truth, back to the author of Truth.

* * *

A Savior has come to save you from sin, not because you are by nature a sinner, but because you have followed a sinner. You have been taught by a sinner.

I want to say to you again that this truth has come to you to separate you from the devil. I am taught by Almighty God, Allah, that he is going to destroy this world. You should try to get out of it, not integrate into it.

II. What the Muslims Want

This is the question asked most frequently by both the whites and the blacks. The answers to this question I shall state as simply as possible.

1. We want freedom. We want a full and complete freedom.

2. We want justice. Equal justice under the law. We want justice applied equally to all, regardless of creed or class or color.

3. We want equality of opportunity. We want equal membership in society with the best in civilized society.

4. We want our people in America whose parents or grandparents were descendants from slaves, to be allowed to establish a separate state or territory of their own—either on this continent or elsewhere. We believe that our former slave-masters are obligated to provide such land and that the area must be fertile and minerally rich. We believe that our former slave-masters are obligated to maintain and supply our needs in this separate territory for the next twenty to twenty-five years—until we are able to produce and supply our own needs.

Since we cannot get along with them in peace and equality, after giving them 400 years of our sweat and blood and receiving in return some of the worst treatment human beings have ever experienced, we believe our contributions to this land and the suffering forced upon us by white America, justifies [sic] our demand for complete separation in a state or territory of our own.

5. We want freedom for all Believers of Islam now held in federal prisons. We want freedom for all black men and women now under death sentence in innumerable prisons in the North as well as the South.

We want every black man and woman to have the freedom to accept or reject being separated from the slave-master's children and establish a land of their own.

We know that the above plan for the solution of the black and white conflict is the best and only answer to the problem between two people.

6. We want an immediate end to the police brutality and mob attacks against the so-called Negro throughout the United States.

We believe that the federal government should intercede to see that black men and women tried in white courts receive justice in accordance with the laws of the land—or allow us to build a new nation for ourselves, dedicated to justice, freedom, and liberty.

7. As long as we are not allowed to establish a state or territory

of our own, we demand not only equal justice under the laws of the United States, but equal employment opportunities—NOW!

We do not believe that after 400 years of free or nearly free labor, sweat, and blood, which has helped America become rich and powerful, that so many thousands of black people should have to subsist on relief, charity or live in poor houses.

8. We want the government of the United States to exempt our people from ALL taxation as long as we are deprived of equal justice under the laws of the land.

9. We want equal education—but separate schools up to sixteen for boys and eighteen for girls on the condition that the girls be sent to women's colleges and universities. We want all black children educated, taught, and trained by their own teachers.

Under such a schooling system we believe we will make a better nation of people. The United States government should provide, free, all necessary textbooks and equipment, schools and college buildings. The Muslim teachers shall be left free to teach and train their people in the way of righteousness, decency, and self respect.

10. We believe that intermarriage or race mixing should be prohibited. We want the religion of Islam taught without hindrance or suppression.

These are some of the things that we, the Muslims, want for our people in North America.

III. Highlights of Messenger's Address, March 28, 1964

War and the So-Called American Negroes' Problem

Should not the ever-increasing threat of universal war, and the scrimmages here and there throughout the world make us, of all people of the earth, be more concerned about our place and future in this war?

We must not forget that the so-called Negroes are still slaves in the hands of white America. We are a long ways from our native land and people. We live in a nation that has not shown us any love or friendship. A people, by nature, who we are as far apart from as the poles.

The so-called Negroes' problem is to find our rightful place in this threatening universal war. Being blind, deaf, and dumb to the knowledge of self have made it impossible for us to find our way to self and our rightful place on this earth, and among our own kind until the coming of Allah (God) in the Person of Master Fard Muhammad.

Integration

Integration is a clever trick of the devils. We should not be deceived by the arch-deceivers in thinking that this offer of integration with them is leading us into a better life than we could ever hope to enjoy.

Integrating with our fathers' slave-masters' children without some of this earth that we can call our own is like merchandise that was once purchased with a price, and now that same merchandise is being returned to the same owner without a price.

Or like a frog that has hopped out of the reach of a snake and settles down, but still in the presence and under the eyes of the snake with the thought that it has hopped far enough to be secure. But the wise snake has his eyes on the frog and is charming it into insensibility, and then the frog is swallowed by the charming snake. The so-called Negroes are being charmed by the white man's promises.

End of the White Man's Rule

We are now living in the time and end of the white race's rule over the original people of earth as predicted by the Divine Prophets of God, and is now being fulfilled by the presence of God in the Person of Master Fard Muhammad. We seek freedom, justice, and equality for our people; and a happy and peaceful future for us on some of this earth that we can call our own as other nations.

We do not care to serve other independent nations. We have served this race for 400 years to maintain their independence here on the original soil of the Red Indians and our black nation. The offer of employment is a poor future for us to depend upon, as the threat of universal war will change the employment situation altogether. Let us seek earth and make employment for ourselves and our children as other nations have done and are doing.

Africa

The preparation that the original black people are making in Africa should be a lesson to the American so-called Negroes. They are making a way for the future of black Africans and not for white Europeans. When the American so-called Negroes learn to love to do something for self, and not so much love and trying to do something for the future of the white race, they will get a place on this earth that they can call their own.

Accept Your Own and Be Yourself

Let us stop trying to be what we are not, and what we are not divinely made to be. If we are to survive and be recognized as members of the civilized people of earth, we must stop loving to intermix into the blood of other than our own kind to destroy not only the morals of our people, but also destroy the entire race and future good of our people.

We have a Brown, Red, and Yellow race, and every one of these is trying to keep his own race's identity. We must use force, if necessary, to stop our people from destroying our race through intermarriages and intermixing—legal or illegal. The most foolish, the most ugly and most ignorant thing the so-called Negroes are doing is falling in love and intermarrying with their slave-masters' children and open enemies who will go to war with each other to keep the so-called Negroes in the status of free slaves. Be yourself and accept your own.

The Fall of America

The disappearance of the rich man, and the worthlessness of the U.S.A.'s currency. A nation is no richer than the value of its money. Europe and America's money has always carried a higher value than Asia's and Africa's currency.

The fall of the value of American currency means the fall of her ruling power. This is the God and glory of the wicked—the American dollar throughout the world. To deprive the wicked of this worship will aid the resurrection of the so-called American Negroes.

Civil Rights

America is making great efforts in the North, East, Middle West, and West to bring about Civil Rights for the so-called Negroes. As you know, the South will never agree 100 per cent because Civil Rights to many of the American whites mean that it will make the ignorant so-called Negroes to not look and think on the better side of this measure such as education and equal opportunity to make a decent living for the poor so-called Negroes.

Instead, he thinks the ignorant so-called Negroes will seek to use this freedom for intermixing and intermarrying with the white man and his woman which is greatly rejected and despised by the southern whites when it comes to a two-way freedom as far as intermarrying and intermixing the blood. I do not think the southern white hates that any more than I or any other intelligent black or white man. No nation that loves the purity of that nation desires any mixture of blood with any un-alike people.

IV. What the Muslims Believe

1. We believe in the One God Whose proper Name is Allah.

2. We believe in the Holy Qur-an and in the Scriptures of all the Prophets of God.

3. We believe in the truth of the Bible, but we believe that it has been tampered with and must be reinterpreted so that mankind will not be snared by the falsehoods that have been added to it.

4. We believe in Allah's Prophets and the Scriptures they brought to the people.

5. We believe in the resurrection of the dead—not in physical resurrection—but in mental resurrection. We believe that the so-called Negroes are most in need of mental resurrection; therefore, they will be resurrected first.

Furthermore, we believe we are the people of God's choice, as it has been written, that God would choose the rejected and the despised. We can find no other persons fitting this description in these last days more than the so-called Negroes in America. We believe in the resurrection of the righteous.

6. We believe in the judgment; we believe this first judgment will take place as God revealed, in America. . . .

7. We believe this is the time in history for the separation of the so-called Negroes and the so-called white Americans. We believe the black man should be freed in name as well as in fact. By this we mean that he should be freed from the names imposed upon him by his former slave-masters. Names which identified him as being the slave-master's slave. We believe that if we are free indeed, we should go in our own people's names—the black peoples of the earth.

8. We believe in justice for all, whether in God or not; we believe as others, that we are due equal justice as human beings. We believe

in equality—as a nation—of equals. We do not believe that we are equal with our slave masters in the status of "freed slaves."

We recognize and respect American citizens as independent peoples and we respect their laws which govern this nation.

9. We believe that the offer of integration is hypocritical and is made by those who are trying to deceive the black peoples into believing that their 400-year-old open enemies of freedom, justice, and equality are, all of a sudden, their "friends." Furthermore, we believe that such deception is intended to prevent black people from realizing that the time in history has arrived for the separation from the whites of this nation.

If the white people are truthful about their professed friendship toward the so-called Negro, they can prove it by dividing up America with their slaves.

We do not believe that America will ever be able to furnish enough jobs for her own millions of unemployed, in addition to jobs for the 20,000,000 black people as well.

10. We believe that we who declared ourselves to be righteous Muslims, should not participate in wars which take the lives of humans. We do not believe this nation should force us to take part in such wars, for we have nothing to gain from it unless America agrees to give us the necessary territory wherein we may have something to fight for.

11. We believe our women should be respected and protected as the women of other nationalities are respected and protected.

12. We believe that Allah (God) appeared in the Person of Master W. Fard Muhammad, July, 1930; the long-awaited "Messiah" of the Christians and the "Mahdi" of the Muslims.

We believe further and lastly that Allah is God and besides HIM there is no God and He will bring about a universal government of peace wherein we all can live in peace together.

Selected Bibliography (Recent Works)

Aptheker, Herbert, *A Documentary History of the Negro People* (New York: Citadel Press, 1951).

Baldwin, James, *Nobody Knows My Name* (New York: Dial Press, 1961). Excellent sketches.

Bardolph, Richard, *The Negro Vanguard* (New York: Holt, Rinehart & Winston, 1959). Based partly on interviews.

Clark, Kenneth B., editor, *The Negro Protest; James Baldwin, Malcolm X, Martin L. King, Jr.* (Boston: Beacon Press, 1963).

World, 1945).

Drake, St. Clair, *Black Metropolis* [Chicago] (New York: Harcourt, Brace &

Du Bois, W. E. B., *Black Folk, Then and Now; an essay in the history and sociology of the Negro race* (New York: Holt, Rinehart & Winston, 1939).

Du Bois, W. E. B., *Dusk of Dawn* (New York: Harcourt, Brace & World, 1940). Autobiographical.

Essien-Udom, E. U., *Black Nationalism* (Chicago: University of Chicago Press, 1963). Analytical.

Franklin, John Hope, *From Slavery to Freedom* (New York: Alfred A. Knopf, 1956). Best survey of Negro history.

Frazier, E. Franklin, *Black Bourgeoisie* (Chicago: Free Press of Glencoe, Illinois, 1957). By a sociologist.

Frazier, E. Franklin, *The Negro in the United States* (New York: The Macmillan Company, 1957). Detailed.

King, Martin Luther, Jr., *Stride Toward Freedom: the Montgomery story* (New York: Harper & Row, Publishers, 1958).

Kugelmass, J. A., *Ralph J. Bunche, Fighter for Peace* (New York: Julian Messner, 1952).

Lincoln, C. Eric, *The Black Muslims in America* (Boston: Beacon Press, 1961). Based on doctoral thesis.

Logan, Rayford W., *The Negro in American Life and Thought* (New York: Dial Press, 1954).

Lomax, Louis E., *The Negro Revolt* (New York: Harper & Row, Publishers, 1962). Stresses mass action as strategy.

McKay, Claude, *Harlem* (New York: E. P. Dutton & Co., 1940).

Meier, August, *The Negro in American Thought, 1880-1915* (Ann Arbor: University of Michigan Press, 1964). Brilliant.

Myrdal, Gunnar, *An American Dilemma* (New York: Harper & Row, Publishers, 1944). Condensed in Arnold Rose, *The Negro in America* (New York: Harper & Row, Publishers, 1948). A classic in race relations; sociological.

Reddick, Lawrence D., *Crusader Without Violence: Martin Luther King, Jr.* (New York: Harper & Row, Publishers, 1959).

Redding, Jay S., *On Being Negro in America* (Indianapolis: Bobbs-Merrill Company, 1951).

Rowan, Carl T., *Go South to Sorrow* (New York: Random House, 1957). By the USIA head; autobiographical.

Rudwick, Elliott M., *W. E. B. Du Bois: A Study in Minority Group Leadership* (Philadelphia: University of Pennsylvania Press, 1960).

Spencer, Samuel R., *Booker T. Washington* (Boston: Little Brown & Co., 1955).

Spero, Sterling D. and Harris, Abram L., *The Black Worker* (Columbia University Press, 1931).

Thompson, Daniel C., *The Negro Leadership Class* (Englewood Cliffs, N. J.: Prentice-Hall, 1963).

Weaver, Robert C., *The Negro Ghetto* (New York: Harcourt, Brace & World, 1948). By the federal housing administrator.

Wesley, Charles H., *Negro Labor in the United States, 1850-1925* (New York: Vanguard, 1927).

Wharton, Vernon L., *The Negro in Mississippi, 1865-1890* (Chapel Hill: University of North Carolina Press, 1947).

White, Walter F., *A Man Called White* (New York: The Viking Press, 1948). By the NAACP leader.

Woodward, C. Vann, *The Strange Career of Jim Crow* (New York: Oxford University Press, 1955). Shows how Jim Crow grew out of formal legislation rather than dominant custom.

The Eyewitness Accounts of American History Series

The American Labor Movement,
edited by Leon Litwack—S-44

American Socialism, 1900-1960,
edited by H. Wayne Morgan—S-85

The Causes of the Civil War,
edited by Kenneth M. Stampp (with revisions)—S-1

The Great Depression,
edited by David A. Shannon—S-10

Immigration as a Factor in American History,
edited by Oscar Handlin—S-2

The Negro Since Emancipation,
edited by Harvey Wish—S-106

The New Deal and the American People,
edited by Frank Freidel—S-87

The Progressive Movement: 1900-1915,
edited by Richard Hofstadter—S-72

Reconstruction, 1865-1877,
edited by Richard N. Current—S-114

Slavery Attacked: The Abolitionist Crusade,
edited by John L. Thomas—S-109

Slavery Defended: The Views of the Old South,
edited by Eric L. McKitrick—S-59

The Twenties: Fords, Flappers and Fanatics,
edited by George E. Mowry—S-69

The Classics in History Series

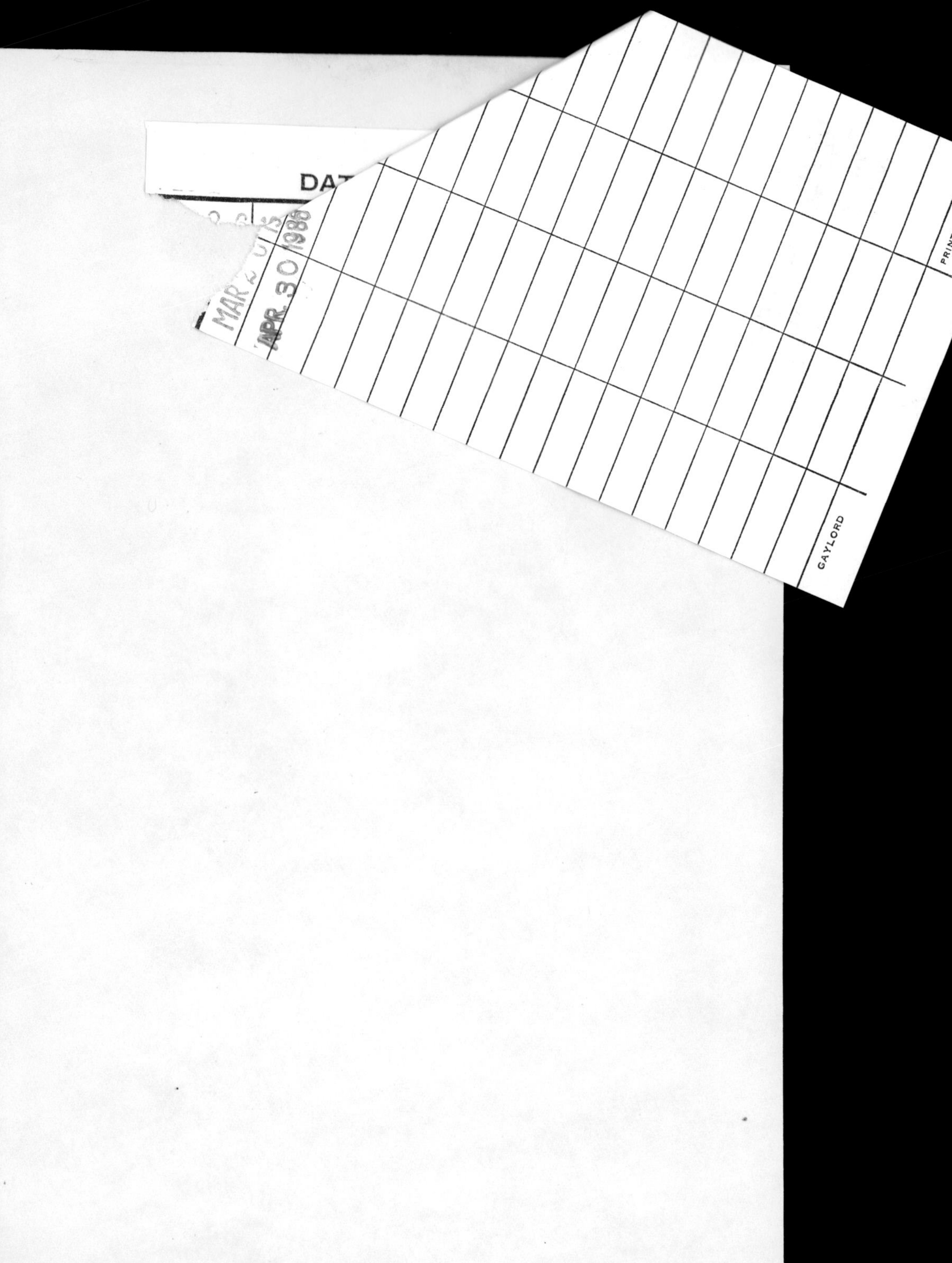
APR. 30 1986
PRINTED IN U.S.A.
GAYLORD